MEN WHO CAN'T LOVE

STEVEN CARTER
and *JULIA SOKOL*

MJF BOOKS
NEW YORK

Published by MJF Books
Fine Communications
POB 0930
Planetarium Station
New York, NY 10024-0540

Library of Congress Catalog Card Number 93-80925
ISBN 1-56731-047-8

Printed by arrangement with M. Evans and Company, Inc.
For information, contact
M. Evans and Company, Inc.
216 East 49 Street
New York, New York 10017

Manufactured in the United States of America

MJF Books and the MJF colophon are trademarks of Fine Creative
Media, Inc.

10 9 8 7 6 5 4 3 2 1

For Carla.

Acknowledgments

As is always the case in a project such as this, there are many people to thank. First and foremost, to all of the men and women who so freely and generously donated their thoughts, feelings, and experiences so that others might benefit, a sincere and heart-felt thank you. Special thanks also to Ronald Fields, Ken Starr, Mary Jane Nolan Kelly, Harold Levinson, Meredith Macrae, Stacey Cahn, Alfred and Sydelle Carter, Peter Coopersmith, and Paddington Coopersmith for their help and advice. Many thanks to the staff at M. Evans, with a very special thank you to George de Kay for giving total support to this project from start to finish. Finally, my greatest thanks to Julia Sokol for her invaluable and immeasurable contribution to this project.

Acknowledgments

Contents

Introduction

Many women have loved a man who cannot love back—a man whose fear of commitment makes him treat her badly, run away, or both. Yet with all that has been written on the subject, most women still don't understand the problem or have any idea what to do about it. Even worse, many women still think this is something that is happening only to them.

I have written this book to make it very clear to women that each of their experiences is not unique. To put it simply, he's not just doing this to *you*, he's done it to *every* woman he's ever been involved with. This book will also enable women to fully understand *why* this happens—to understand what it is about a committed relationship that frightens some men so, and how that fear often leads to bizarre, confusing, and contradictory behavior patterns. But most important, this book will enable women to do something about it.

It is easy for women to blame themselves for attracting this kind of man and thus accept full responsibility for the problem. This is a terrible mistake. The reason so many women get involved with these men is not because they have some subconscious desire to punish themselves. Nor is it because there is some weakness in their character. It is because so many of the men they meet have this problem. While many of these men will ultimately manage to overcome their fears, some will *never* be able to make a commitment, regardless of the circumstances.

It is crucial that women understand and accept this and learn to recognize and avoid these worst-case scenarios.

I think that most of the confusion and misunderstanding among women is the result of a one-sided approach to the commitment problem. What I mean is that all too often, men's fear of commitment is approached and interpreted entirely from the female perspective, and advice is then offered from that perspective. But this is a problem that starts in *men's* minds, not women's, and it can only be solved by getting inside men's minds and exposing it.

But don't get me wrong. If it seems as though I spend the bulk of this book talking about *him* and *his* problem, it is not because I want you to lose sight of *your* needs—this happens all too often, and is a terrible mistake. Nor is it because I want you to feel sorry for him, pity him, or worry about him—I don't. Nor is it because I want you to change him or be his therapist —only a professional can help *him*.

I'm giving you this information to help *you*—to help you help yourself. You see, in order to do something about the commitment problem *you* must understand exactly what is going on inside his head. Without this insight you may be forever at his mercy, but with it, you will have the tools you need to know what is happening and to take control of your life and the life of your relationship. Then, and only then, will you be capable of having the kind of love you need and deserve.

Part 1
HIS PROBLEM

Chapter 1

THE COMMITMENT PROBLEM

Here's the problem: Many men have an exaggerated fear of commitment. If you are a contemporary woman, there is a very good chance that you are going to be involved with at least one man, possibly more, who chooses to walk away from love. It may be the man who doesn't call after a particularly good first date; it may be the ardent pursuer who woos you only to leave after the first night of sex; it may be the trusted boyfriend and lover who sabotages the relationship just as it heads for marriage, or it may be the man who waits until after marriage to respond to the enormity of his commitment by ignoring your emotional needs and becoming unfaithful or abusive. However, whenever it happens, chances are you are dealing with a man who has an abnormal response to the notion of commitment. To *him* something about *you* spells out wife, mother, togetherness—*forever*—and it terrifies him. That's why he leaves you. You don't understand it. You don't see yourself as threatening. As a matter of fact, you may not even have wanted that much from this particular guy. If it's any consolation, he probably doesn't understand his reactions any better than you do. All he knows is that the relationship is "too close for comfort." Something about it, and therefore you, makes him anxious.

If his fear is strong enough, this man will ultimately sabotage, destroy, or run away from any solid, good relationship. He wants love, but he is terrified—genuinely phobic—about commitment and will run away from any woman who represents "happily ever after." In other words, if his fear is too great, the commitment-phobic will not be able to love, no matter how much he wants to.

But that's not how it seems at the beginning. At the beginning of the relationship, when you look at him you see a man who seems to need and want love. His blatant pursuit and touching displays of vulnerability convince you that it is "safe" for you to respond in kind. But as soon as you do, as soon as you are willing to give love a chance, as soon as it's time for the relationship to move forward, something changes. Suddenly the man begins running away, either figuratively, by withdrawing and provoking arguments, or literally, by disappearing and never calling again. Either way, you are left with disappointed dreams and destroyed self-esteem. What happened, what went wrong, and why is this scenario so familiar to so many women?

"ONE DAY HE SAID WE WERE PERFECT TOGETHER—THE NEXT WE WEREN'T TOGETHER. WHAT HAPPENED?"

Jamie has very vivid recollections of the way she felt on the day she met Michael.

"I had just turned twenty-eight, and although there wasn't a man in my life, I felt pretty pleased about everything else. I had just finished my first week at a brand new job—administrative assistant with a major ballet company—and I loved it because I love dance. I had a rent-controlled studio apartment with a bay window, and just enough extra money in my wallet to treat myself to a Mostly Mozart concert. After the concert, my ex-roommate had invited me to a party. I almost didn't go. Anyway, that's where I met Michael. I was wearing this long pink and white skirt with an overblouse, and he came up to me and said, 'You look just like an ice cream cone.' "

Jamie says that something about the directness of Michael's approach made her back off and avoid him for the rest of the evening, but when she got home, there was a message from him on her answering machine asking if she would be free for brunch the following day. She decided to ignore it. It wasn't that Michael wasn't attractive—he was. But he wasn't her type. He was a little too "yuppie" for her—too smooth, too comfortable with himself—to tell the truth, too arrogant.

He called the next day when she was out doing her laundry and left another message. Before she had time to think about it, the phone rang. It was him. "Okay," he said, "how about dinner tonight?" When she said she was busy, he suggested brunch on Sunday. She said she couldn't. Then, worried that she might have been rude, she started to make small talk. They ended up staying on the phone for fifteen minutes. She doesn't remember what they talked about, except that it was funny, and she learned that he was a very highly paid advertising copy-writer.

"I thought about it a lot during the week and wondered whether I had made a mistake in not going out with him. It wasn't as though I was surrounded by good-looking men pleading to buy me dinner—I hadn't even had a date for at least six months. I decided that as usual I was being too picky, too choosy. That Friday I went to a movie with a friend who whined the whole time about where she and her boyfriend should spend their joint vacation. Saturday I stayed home, watched 'The Golden Girls,' and felt sorry for myself."

I have discovered that many women worry that they may be turning down their last chance at love. Jamie was no different, and when Michael called again the following Wednesday, she didn't say no, and they met for dinner. He surprised her by being very open about his life as well as interested in hearing about hers. His sensitivity was very touching. Until recently, Michael said, he had been seeing a woman who was more in-volved with her career and co-op conversion than she was with him. When he settled down, Michael said, he wanted a woman like Jamie who had her priorities in order. She was pleased that he admired her priorities, but she wondered how he knew what they were. He said he realized it was time for him to think about getting a dog and a station wagon and a wife—"not necessarily in that order." He said he knew that's what would give him the incentive to spend more time on creative writing and less on advertising. He told Jamie that he thought it was charming that she used to write music. "Maybe if it works out between us, we'll end up in a big Victorian house in the suburbs. I can write the Great American Novel in the library, and you can play our grand piano in the living room." Jamie didn't bother telling him that her interest was in hard rock, but she was charmed by the thought.

"When Michael said good night, he asked me if I liked the beach. Well, I love the beach, so we made a date for Sunday. He was so attentive that day. He put suntan lotion on my shoulders, took me out beyond the breakers and made sure I could handle all the waves . . . I'm from the Midwest and I'm not used to the ocean. Afterward we went to a small off-beat restaurant frequented by locals. He said it had great clam sauce, and it did. It had tables near the water and I loved it. Michael was so totally attentive it made me self-conscious. He even buttered my bread for me. He played with my hair, kissed my neck when nobody was looking, and made me feel totally irresistible."

It goes without saying that when they got back to her apartment, he wanted to stay the night. But Jamie resisted, even when Michael argued that they had spent so much time together in one day and had said so much that it was as if they had been dating for more than a month. But Jamie still didn't believe that he was as interested in her as he said he was. She didn't think she was really his type.

He had to go out of town briefly that week, but he called her from his hotel room every night, talking for hours. She thinks that's when she began to trust his pursuit. He made a date for Friday night. By the time dinner was finished, it was apparent that he was coming home with her, and that's where they stayed until Sunday morning.

"There is no question in my mind. I started being seriously interested in Michael because he seemed seriously interested in me. I was overwhelmed by the level of emotional intimacy he gave and expected. And I liked it—it made me feel safe and secure. I think when it ended that was what I missed. I definitely wasn't as swept away by the sex as Michael seemed to be—he was just more continuously passionate than me—but I certainly didn't let him know that. How could I? He kept saying, 'You're perfect. I can't get over how perfect we are together.' Besides, I was falling in love, and I assumed that once my body and my emotions connected, everything would be just fine. He must have told me about everything in his life, from his relationships with his best friends to his problems with his father and his dissatisfactions at work. I didn't realize it at the time, but I was beginning to be the expert on Michael's life. By the time the relationship was over, I think I knew and remembered more about his life than he did. When he left that Sunday night I thought it was the beginning of something real.

"He didn't call me every night as he had the week before. Instead he called me every day, at work. A subtle shift, and not one I actually paid much attention to. Once again, he said he couldn't see me during the week—he had business, and previous plans, and a million and one things to do—but once again he arrived on Friday, and once again we crawled into bed, ate Chinese food out of containers, and he talked himself silly. Saturday night, we watched a movie on TV, and someplace in the middle of it, I got up to get him a Coke. When I handed it to him, he looked at me very intently and said, 'I'm falling in love with you.' By the time we went to sleep, he was braver about the whole thing. He said, 'I love you.' He seemed to like me so much that it outweighed any reservations I might have had. I remember thinking that maybe I was finally mature enough to appreciate a man who genuinely liked me. At that moment I felt very fortunate to be loved, and I was prepared to love him, to do whatever I could to make him happy, and to get on with the business of living. I was wondering if he would get along with my friends, and if I would get along with his parents. I guess I was naive, but to me love means that marriage is being thought about. Love goes with marriage, love and marriage. It didn't occur to me that it wasn't connected. I was thinking about the future; it didn't even occur to me that the relationship was already on a downhill path.

"Then, Sunday morning, he got up and said he had to leave because his roommates were having some people over for brunch and he had to be there. I wondered why he didn't ask me to come with him, but I didn't want to overreact. I also didn't want to be demanding or nagging—I wanted a relationship built on mutual trust and respect. You have to understand, though, that it made me feel bad. It's amazing. We went out together for five months, and I never did get to meet his roommates."

On this weekend Michael established the pattern that was to continue for the next couple of months. He would call Jamie every day at work and make a date for the weekend. He would arrive on Friday night, and they would spend most of the weekend hanging out and making love. Sometimes they would go out for a movie or dinner, but as Jamie remembers it, most of the time was spent in the apartment.

"Michael kept telling me that he was exhausted from work, that I was his refuge—the only person or thing he wanted to be with. Also, you have to understand, the sex by now was terrific, terrific intimate sex. I trusted the sex, the intimacy, and the friendship. He told me everything about himself. He said I made him feel happy. I was perfect. We were perfect, cozy, close and perfect."

During that time, Jamie met only one of Michael's friends, once for a quick drink, and she thinks that may have been an accident. One Friday his mother, who lived in Connecticut, was staying over in New York, and Michael had dinner with her. Jamie thought she should have been invited, but Michael said that his parents were really difficult about accepting new women, and he wanted to prepare them. Then suddenly it was Thanksgiving, the first of the holidays. Michael kept telling her they were a couple, but Jamie knew that what happened over the holidays would be a clear indication of how much a couple they were.

"He went to his parents' and didn't invite me. I was crushed. He was obviously feeling guilty because he came over on the Wednesday before with a bottle of wine and some flowers.

He said he felt awful about leaving me alone. 'So don't leave,' I said. 'If you really think your parents won't accept me, why can't you just stay with me? You're an adult, stay with me. Make me the priority.' He said he couldn't do that.

"What made it even more disgusting is that he was redoing his résumé, and I had agreed to type it on the word processor in my office, and I had to do that on the Friday after Thanksgiving. He was coming back on Monday, and I expected him to call immediately. He didn't. He didn't call until Wednesday, when he asked if I wanted to join him for coffee. I noticed this because he had never before seen me in the middle of the week if he had work the next day. I thought it might indicate that he had thought about the relationship and was prepared to give it more time. He came over to my apartment, picked up his résumé, and we ended up in bed. He said he had to go home to sleep because he didn't have clothes. At the door he said, 'I love you.' He didn't say anything about the weekend. Neither did I. I just took it for granted. But I was getting concerned. I planned to confront him when I saw him—but when we had more time to talk it out. Friday rolled around, and he didn't call to make plans. I started calling girlfriends asking what I should do. The universal advice was to sit tight because I shouldn't look too anxious. Besides, he might just be in a meeting or something. But he didn't call.

"I'll never forget how I felt that Friday after work. I guess I knew the relationship was over, but I couldn't accept it. Why had we ended up in bed Wednesday if that was the case? I also—and I know this sounds stupid, but it's what I was thinking—was worried that something was wrong with him. By ten o'clock I couldn't stand it, so I called his apartment. Of course, his machine answered. I hung up, then I got embarrassed thinking that he would know it was me and called again and left a message. When he phoned, on Saturday, he said he knew he should have called me but he had been too busy to call, and now he had to go back up to Connecticut because his parents had obligated him for a family party. I was sufficiently intimidated not to suggest his taking me. He said he would call me when he returned, and he did, on Sunday. As a matter of fact, he came over. As usual, it was

warm and wonderful between us. He fell asleep in front of
the television, and I hung his jacket up. When I did, I couldn't
help but notice a Playbill sticking out of the pocket. It was
for a theater in New York, and it was for the night before.
That's how I found out that he was not in Connecticut, and
that he was also lying to me."

From this point on, Michael established a new pattern. It was
called 'anything goes.' Some days he would call. Others he didn't.
He continued to ask Jamie to see him, but not on a regular basis
or schedule.

"He told me he was very busy at work and genuinely stressed
by the strain it put on him. The first week after Thanksgiving,
he saw me on a Friday and went home on the Saturday. The
following week, he saw me on Saturday and went home right
after dinner, with a totally garbled excuse. Through this all,
he kept telling me he loved me, and asking me to bear with
him just a bit longer. Whenever he came over, I found myself
going to amazing lengths to prepare special treats and to look
good. I didn't know what to do to get him back to where we
had been. It might have stretched out longer, but Christmas
was coming up fast. I couldn't afford the time or the money
to go home, and I didn't want to be alone, so I guess I made
demands that he couldn't accept. I wanted to know that we
would spend the holidays together. He couldn't commit to it.
He told me he realized he was being unfair but he didn't know
what he wanted. He was feeling very unsettled. He blamed
the situation at work. He said he needed time to think about
'things.' I asked him if he was seeing someone else. He said
no, but I didn't believe him.

"Finally, the week before Christmas, we met at my insist-
ence, and I asked him what had happened between us. He
said that 'artistic types were a little too weird' for him to
handle, and that he had to get away from my intensity. Trust
me, I had never done anything remotely weird. I tried to get
him to talk about it and he wouldn't; he just kept saying I was
too intense.

"He called me one more time to wish me a merry Christmas, and then after he hung up, I got so angry that I phoned

him back and screamed at him. He said he couldn't talk to
me when I was so much out of control. I would have asked
him to see me so I could tell him in person how upset I felt,
but I was afraid he would say no. After we hung up, I felt
guilty about screaming. I wanted to apologize. Even though
I knew better, I worried that I hadn't been sufficiently understanding and that now I *had* been weird and intense, and
he really had an excuse to reject me. I wanted to call back,
but I was afraid he would hang up on me. And that was it. It
was over."

AFTER IT'S OVER

As Jamie was quick to tell me, she went through a lot of pain
because of this relationship. The fact that the end came over the
holidays didn't help. She says that her mind was in a constant
obsessive whir. She couldn't accept the fact that "her" Michael,
the one who had told her that he loved her, could have treated
her that way, so she looked for other people to blame. She
blamed his friends. She blamed his childhood and his relationship with his parents. But mostly she blamed herself. She knew
that Michael had trouble trusting anyone. She should have worked
harder to build his trust before she confronted him. But then
again, maybe she confronted him too late. If she had said something that first Sunday when he went off to brunch and didn't
include her, perhaps the whole pattern of the relationship would
have been different.

Maybe he never really liked her. Maybe she really wasn't his
physical type. Then again, maybe that's all she was—his physical
type. Maybe all he wanted to do was sleep with her. When she
thought about it, that didn't make sense either. As a matter of
fact, nothing made sense to Jamie except that she felt miserable.
She remembered all the things he had said to her at the beginning, and decided that it had to be something about her that
had turned him off. Maybe if she changed that, she might be
able to get him back. But then again, he had turned out to be
so unkind. Why would she want him back?

"I felt totally betrayed by Michael. He told me he loved
me, and I believed him, and I thought that love meant some-

thing. The fact that it didn't left me with so much pain that I didn't know what to do. I went out and bought every book on relationships I could get my hands on. I had one friend who had been through a similar experience, and we spent hours together on the phone obsessing over the details of every conversation each of us had had with our respective men. Finally I went into therapy, which, by the way, I couldn't afford. But nothing really made any sense. Also, by the way, I have to mention that I stopped talking to some of my friends. Often when I tried to tell people what had happened, they looked at me as though I was exaggerating both the intensity of his pursuit and the intensity of his rejection. It made me feel embarrassed and pathetic. But I just didn't understand how he could have told me he loved me and treated me this way."

Jamie told me that she kept thinking that somewhere there was a secret, and that if she had the key she could find an explanation that made sense. But what was it? Why did Michael change? Why did he treat her so badly? How could a sensitive man behave with such cruelty? How could a man who seemed to like her so much change so totally toward her? What happened? What went wrong? Why did it end? Why did he run away from love?

MY STORY

Before I could answer those questions, I had to examine my own relationships with women, and it seems fitting that I should be the first man in this book to admit to feelings of commitmentphobia. When my last relationship ended, I couldn't help but be aware that something was acutely wrong with the way I was conducting myself with women. Many of my excuses for not being in a committed relationship suddenly didn't hold water. They worked when I was twenty; they worked at twenty-five; but when I passed thirty, they weren't working anymore. What I had been able to view as isolated incidents and silly little events from my past had begun to emerge as a life pattern. And I knew it was time to do something about it.

My belated self-examination was probably speeded up by several coincidences in both my professional and personal lives. Ironically, when my last relationship started to disintegrate, I was on a book tour assuming the role of interpersonal guru— ironic because I was beginning to have as many questions as I had answers.

The audiences I was addressing were composed mostly of women. This is fairly typical because, as everyone knows, women tend to be more interested in discussing relationships. Women also tend to ask more questions, and they open up more and are less threatened by self-evaluation. Many of these women were openly upset, and several of them told me that they were trying to recover from involvements with men who ran away from the possibility of real commitment. They were experiencing so many emotions that I often felt as though I was being confronted with an avalanche of feelings.

I remember many of these women and their stories vividly. Several told me long, complicated tales of men who had pressured and pursued them into making some sort of emotional commitment. When the women finally said yes, the guys either backed away or began to employ destructive hurtful behavior to sabotage the relationship. Many told me of idyllic dates and weekends and long-range plans with ardent men who suddenly pulled away with no warning. Some of these men only moved away emotionally; others actually stopped calling and disappeared so totally that several women joked about having a mock wake for all the men who certainly must have died. They could find no other explanation for behavior that was not only bizarre and unpredictable, but downright insensitive and cruel.

I liked talking to these women. It was terrific being viewed as Mr. Sensitive, Mr. Understanding, Mr. Nice Guy, but it was a hoax. When I stopped to think about my own relationships, I couldn't help but acknowledge that there had been times when I was no different from most of the "creeps" they complained about. I had never given any relationship my best shot. There was no question about it in my mind: My behavior made it clear that I was afraid of commitment. I had never managed to make a serious try at it. Oh sure, I gave it lip service, but when I thought about it, I had to admit that there had been times when

I had found a reason why a perfectly suitable woman was unacceptable—a flimsy excuse for ending the relationship.

THE FLIMSY EXCUSE FOR NOT COMMITTING—A COMMOM THREAD

I thought about all the times I had talked to men about sex, love, and relationships, and all the excuses I had heard from my male friends about why a woman was unacceptable or a relationship had to end—"too demanding," "too short," "too tall," "too heavy," "what if she turned out to be anorexic?" "she had a difficult mother," "she had a difficult child," "she had a difficult cat," "she had the wrong career," "she had the same career," she had, she was, etc., etc. I thought about all the men I knew personally and professionally, as well as the men who had come to me for advice after my first book was published. It seemed inconceivable, but was it possible that all these "unhappy" men—the ones who found so many reasons for why a particular relationship had to end, why they couldn't find the woman of their dreams, why they had never been able to make a permanent commitment—were the very same men the women I was meeting were complaining about? Were all of the complaints I heard merely a means of masking a deep fear of commitment? Were all of these men who I always found myself feeling sorry for really "wolves in sheep's clothing?"

WHAT MEN SAY, AND WHAT MEN DO—THE CONTRADICTION

A major complaint on the part of women: He says one thing and he does another. So many women mentioned this contradiction that I decided to examine it more closely. Certainly it was true of many single men I knew. We say we want nothing more than to settle down in a happy marriage, but that's not what we are doing. Why? I didn't think I was alone in realizing that I concocted elaborate rationalizations and reasons for not going forward with a particular relationship, but I decided to find out for sure. I decided to ask men to tell me the truth. I wanted straight answers, and I thought I knew how to get them. But before I could talk to men, I felt I needed to hear from women themselves precisely what it was they were complaining about. When I interviewed the men, I wanted to be able to be specific. How did the women feel that they had been treated unfairly, and what did they think was going on? I had to talk to women first.

TALKING TO WOMEN

I began by interviewing approximately fifty single women. All of the women were attractive, desirable, contemporary women who had a lot to offer any man. I tried to interview equal numbers of single, divorced, and married women so that I would not get a slanted point of view. Also, I chose women from different parts of the country and in different economic brackets. I collected their stories of relationships and situations experienced first-hand. Some of these tales were quite extreme. I listened, trying not to look shocked as women talked about men they trusted who did the old disappearing act, vanishing in the night, disappearing almost in a puff of smoke. I heard two separate stories of men who had ended relationships by walking out while the woman was in the shower, and never phoning again. One woman told me that her fiancé walked out of a Rome hotel room for a pack of cigarettes and never returned. In all of these cases, there had been no arguments, no harsh words. So many women told me of men who pulled out of marriage plans that I lost track. One woman told me that the man she expected to marry joined the Peace Corps as the event drew closer and actually left for Bangkok two days before they were to be married. May I emphasize, he went by himself. Others told me of relationships in which ardent pursuers turned into silent, angry enemies as soon as the woman agreed to do one of the following: move in, marry, have children.

All of these women basically spoke to the same issue: an abandonment and betrayal of trust that had taken place in a relationship in which they had been encouraged, by the man, to expect tender intimacy.

TALKING TO MEN

Armed with these stories and confidences, I started to interview men. The first men I talked to were intelligent, normal guys. I used the same criteria as I had for the women. Many of them were well educated. Most paid lip service to the women's movement. For the most part they were men who claimed to be sensitive to women's issues. The question: Were these average, well-brought-up, smart men who were treating women so badly? What were they doing, and how were they doing it? And, most important, why?

Here are some of the things I wanted to know: When they entered a relationship, did they have a hidden agenda? Did they purposely manipulate? Did they know that they were frightened of permanent commitment? Did that fear make them anticipate and provoke the dissolution of a relationship by finding excuses as to why it couldn't continue?

I also wanted answers to specifics: Had any of these men pursued a woman and then stopped calling her once they had slept together? Had any of them proposed to women only to change their minds at the last minute? Why, and what did they do then? Had any of them moved in with a woman, become afraid of the commitment, and responded with rage at his entrapment—the proverbial caged beast, angry and abusive toward the woman he perceived as his captor? Did men behave this way in order to distance themselves? Did they do it in order to sabotage relationships, so that either the women would call it quits or the stage would be set for their own departure? Did any of them become unfaithful whenever the relationship got too good, too close? Had they ever run away from a woman with whom they were closely and intimately involved, a woman who had every reason to expect marriage, and/or better treatment? Did any one of them wine, dine, and charm so many women that no one woman could possibly stand a chance of getting his affection? Did many of them consistently choose women who were inappropriate for them, women with whom there was always an automatic excuse for getting out and not moving forward?

I don't know what I expected. But I was shocked by what

men told me. It wasn't that I hadn't believed the women's versions of their involvement with commitmentphobic men. But somehow I had thought it would be different types of men, aberrations, not the kind of men I knew. I was wrong. I discovered that some of the men I thought I knew well had been telling me partial truths about the direction their relationships had taken and how and why they ended. I came away from the first group of interviews absolutely convinced of three things:

■ When a relationship gets too close, men who fear commitment often behave in a totally irrational fashion.

■ These men look for excuses and faults in the woman to help them feel better about their behavior.

■ Most of these men know deep down that their constant emphasis on negatives is only a means of rationalizing that allows them to avoid looking too deeply at their own major flaw—the inability to commit.

"I DON'T WANT TO TALK ABOUT THIS NOW"—HOW MEN PRESERVE THEIR MYSTIQUE

A great many books have been written which attempt to advise women who are alone or in unsatisfactory relationships. I have read virtually all of these books, and it seems to me that there is a plethora of lopsided information. Most of these books and articles are based solely on interviews with women or on extremely superficial interviews with men.

I wrote this book for women because I wanted to give them insight into how men think, and I wanted to help them understand the commitment problem. In order to do this, I felt I needed to get the truth from as many men as possible. When I started out to do this, I began to understand the enormity of the problem. These men are difficult. They are almost impossible to pin down, and they don't want to talk about this subject. The common response: "I don't want to talk about this now." Sure, they will answer a few simple survey questions or give superficial information, but that's it. Many of the men I spoke to felt genuinely guilty. They didn't want to think about what they did or what motivated them to do it.

If I had not been so determined it would have been impossible to get as many in-depth interviews as I got. I did what many women wished they could do: I tracked guys down, flushed them out of their lairs, made light of all their rationalizations, and got them to tell me what really happened. At some points it became quite funny. Some of them stopped returning my phone calls. Several had to be called ten or fifteen times just to get a five-minute interview. I interviewed men who "couldn't talk now" in their cars on their way to work. Tape recorder in hand, I chased one guy around his apartment while he packed. I went with men on their dates. I bribed them by agreeing to give tennis lessons. I even washed one guy's car.

I was absolutely determined that I was not going to end up with a bunch of superficial interviews with guys. But it wasn't easy getting these men to break through the surface and talk. If nothing else, the experience gave me a very clear understanding of how hard it is for women to get straight answers from men who are in conflict about commitment.

"I'M PROBABLY TO BLAME HERE"—HOW WOMEN HELP MAINTAIN THE MYTH

Women, on the other hand, were not only all too willing to break through the surface, they were willing to assume responsibility for the whole problem. The vast majority of them were totally different in attitude from the men. When these women talked about the men in their lives, almost all of them tried to emphasize the man's best qualities. They seemed always to look for valid reasons, even if it meant accepting blame, for intolerable male behavior. They were almost always trying to make something work, even when it wasn't working.

I don't honestly think this difference in attitude is totally the result of accident or of biology. It seems fair to mention current popular nonfiction and the degree of responsibility that is given to women for their role in the disturbed social scene.

Think about it: Nice, smart, good-looking women are considering analysis because they "love too much." I have seen no similar suggestions that might induce men into therapy because they "love too little." As to smart women making foolish choices, in the real world, this is not what's going on. These women are not doing the choosing. They are being chosen. And it's not because they are giving off peculiar, neurotic-type signals. It's because they are attractive, intelligent women who attract men. The problem is that so many of the men they are attracting suffer from the same problem—the commitment problem.

THE MAN WHO CAN'T LOVE: When He Runs and the Woman Wonders Why

If you have heard as many stories as I have, you can't help but notice that all commitmentphobic relationships have a common dynamic, and they end in ways that are eerily similar. Typically, the man exhibits readily identifiable behavior. His overall pattern falls into what I call the "pursuit/panic syndrome." All that really means is that the guy does a one-thousand-degree pursuit until he feels that the woman's love and response leaves him no way out of the relationship—*ever*. The moment that happens, he begins to perceive the relationship as a trap. That trap provokes anxiety, if not total panic. Before the woman knows what is happening, the man is running from the relationship, running from her, and running from love.

In these relationships, there are usually very distinct stages and very distinct patterns within each stage. The major variable is how long each stage lasts. Some men can go through all the stages of the pursuit/panic syndrome in the course of one night. Others take years.

There are men who have a good first date and don't call again because they are immediately concerned about the expectation of marriage. To others, sex spells commitment. For many, it is the moment the relationship becomes sticky, which, to such a man, means he is getting stuck.

It goes without saying that a woman can be devastated by such a man. The depth of her unhappiness is partially dependent upon how far into the relationship they progressed before he hit the panic button. The only common denominator is that the man has rarely been giving the woman clear signals, and she rarely expects him to leave her. She usually has a sense that something has happened in the man's head, but she doesn't know what has triggered his need to get out.

When a man runs depends upon what he perceives as the commitment point of no return. This moment is dependent upon several factors, including the man's pattern, the woman's behavior, and the degree of involvement. Whenever it happens, it is a turning point, the moment when the man looks at a particular woman and feels that if he doesn't get out immediately, he will be trapped forever.

If he is going to panic, he usually does so at one of four different points in the relationship.

THE COMMITMENT POINTS OF NO RETURN
Point 1: One Date, No More

Every woman has lost a few men at point one. This happens when the commitmentphobic has an exceptionally good first date and decides not to call back.

Renee T. recalls:

"I know this is crazy. It was only one real date. But it was a perfect one—a day spent on the water on a friend's boat. We moored near a private beach and went swimming. We ate lobsters on a pier. It was the most intensely intimate day you can imagine. He said he never felt more at peace than he did with me. He told me over and over again how beautiful he thought I was. We didn't spend the night together because I had to go home to my daughter, but I went to bed expecting him to call first thing the next morning to pick up where we left off. He has never asked me out again. For a long time I thought it was because of something I said. This is really crazy, but it gives you some idea of how confused I was . . . At one point during that day, I looked up at him—he's six three— and said, 'Gee, you're tall.' I meant it as a compliment. But I was so convinced that I had done something that I thought maybe I made him self-conscious and he started hating me for it. I couldn't believe somebody would behave the way he did."

Point 2: A Don Juan Look-Alike Contest

When a man sleeps with a woman once and starts to back away, he is panicking at Point 2. He may call a woman again after the first date, but the sex immediately starts to deteriorate. (He is easily mistaken for a classic Don Juan, but don't let the superficial resemblance confuse you.)

Anne B. recalls:

"The best part of this story is that the guy was an Anglican priest, if you can believe this. He lived in Philadelphia. I lived in New York, but we had friends in common and music in common. For whatever it is worth, we were also the same religion. We were both vacationing near a music festival and we spent a couple of weeks in close contact. By the end of the first week, he was telling me how important I was to him. He actually told me he was falling in love with me. He also, I should add, spent a lot of time talking about the importance of values and commitment and all that sort of stuff. Well, we finally got back to New York, and instead of going straight to Philadelphia, he came home with me, and I agreed to go to bed with him. I was quite smitten. He left the next morning. He said he would call me the next day, but he didn't call for two weeks. By the time he did, I knew it was not going to work out, and he sounded very distant and strange. I tried phoning him several times, and I sent him a couple of post-cards and, I'm ashamed to admit, a little birthday present, but he never called me again. I was devastated. I blamed the fact that I lived in a different city. I wrote him several long letters, which friends fortunately talked me out of sending, in which I assumed responsibility for the sins of the world. How could a man who spent so much time talking about right and wrong behave so badly? I was sure for at least a year that I must have done something. I still think about him some-times."

Point 3: Almost Home

Point 3 is where most men panic. Up until this point, the man appears to be trying to develop a real relationship. By point

3, all the preliminaries are finished, and it's time for the relationship to move forward. He bails out because he fears getting stuck.

Lori S. recalls:

"We lived in different cities. He was in Boston; I was in New York, so for two years we only saw each other on weekends and for vacations. Our phone bills were outrageous. He kept proposing and asking me to be with him. Finally I agreed. I found a new job; he found the apartment. He was supposed to move in with me within a month or two. I had been in the apartment for two weeks—the books were still in cartons—when he changed. First he started putting off when he was going to move. Then he started not showing up when he was supposed to—he would always be late. I thought he was just having commitment jitters, but we had been together for so long, I didn't think we would ever break up. One night, I was making him a special birthday dinner when he called. He said he didn't feel well and wouldn't be over. I asked him if he wanted me to pack up dinner and bring it to his apartment. 'No,' he said. I could hear voices in the background. I was so upset that I went over to his apartment. He wasn't home. I phoned him at half-hour intervals all night long. He never came home. When I reached him at work the next day, he admitted he had been with someone else. Well, we split up immediately, but then we patched it up again. We went back and forth this way for a month or so, but it became more and more obvious that he couldn't go through with our plans. He was clearly seeing other women, and it got really ugly. I went into analysis to try and get over him, and eventually was able to get free emotionally."

Point 4: The Morning After

By point 4, a formal commitment has been made, and the relationship has all of the superficial characteristics of permanency. When a man panics at point 4, it is usually the most devastating.

Carole R. recalls:

"When I married Bob, I thought that I had finally gotten

lucky. This was my second marriage—my kids were grown. Bob was wonderful to me; he said he adored me. He couldn't wait until we got married, and he promised he would make up for all the problems that went before. Well, in truth, he started getting a little different a couple of days before the ceremony. For example, he complained that my older daughter hadn't smiled at him when she walked into the house— small stuff. But before there had never been anything wrong with me or anything about me, including children, friends, work. But within days after we were married, he started to find fault with me. By the end of the first year, there was nothing about me that was right. I would try to change, but that didn't stop him—he would just find something else. He didn't stop. The way I walked, the way I talked, the way I did dishes. When I walked into the room, he would look unhappy. He also started getting sick. He must have had the flu for four straight months. I had been through something like this before, and I could see that he just couldn't handle marriage. But I think, because he had been so insistent before he wanted me to be the one to break the relationship. When I noticed that he was looking at other women, I asked for a separation. I think that if I had been just a little younger, or a little more insecure, I would have been wiped out."

AFTER THE RELATIONSHIP—KNOWING THAT IT'S NOT YOUR FAULT

The woman who gets involved with one of these men *also* has a typical response. When the relationship begins, chances are she is not as interested as the man and is won over by the intensity of his interest in her. At the end, she is totally confused.

All of the women I talked to voiced some concern that something they may have said or done threw the man over the edge. If they confronted the man and asked for a commitment, they blamed themselves for precipitating his withdrawal. If they failed to confront, they blamed themselves for allowing the man to set up a relationship style that was doomed to disintegrate or drift off into never-never land. Even though they knew intellectually that they had not been guilty of sabotaging the relationship, each woman couldn't help but look for a rational explanation and wonder whether it was something she did—or neglected to do—that set the man off.

But in most cases, nothing went wrong in the relationship. In fact, part of the problem is that he backs off when things are going *too* well. You see, the only thing wrong is that this man simply cannot make a commitment. Therefore when he thinks he perceives "C"-Day approaching (a perception that may have little or nothing to do with reality), he suddenly does a 180-degree turn, stops pursuing, starts running away, and in some cases quite literally drops out of sight.

The Situation Is Not the Woman's Fault, but It Has Become Her Problem

In an ideal world, a woman would only have to continue doing what many of them *are* doing—being warm, kind, attractive, smart, accomplished, and sympathetic—and men would flock to her side. I'm sorry, but this is not what's happening. Terrific women are not having terrific relationships with terrific men. These women respond to this by shaking their heads and thinking they have to be more terrific—perfectly sane, perfectly loving, perfectly terrific—in short, perfect. I don't think this is going to work. Here's why: What these men fear is commitment, and when they look at you and your perfection, they know that you are someone to marry and live with happily ever after. This is precisely what they don't want to do—so, they run in the other direction. This is not your fault, but it certainly has become your problem.

But the situation is far from hopeless; it is not all black-and-white. With many men, it's a question of degree. If you're a woman who is involved with one of these men, or who is worried about what tomorrow will bring, I think there is a great deal you can do to protect yourself and change the future of your relationships with men. But first you have to understand the problem, and you have to be able to know when you are involved with such a man. You also have to understand how many of the ways you have been programmed to behave can exacerbate the problem. You can protect yourself in relationships with men who fear commitment by learning to:

1. Identify the man who can't love (and the degree of his problem) *before* you get involved.

2. Determine whether or not a man can ever change.

3. Determine whether or not he is worth the trouble.

4. Desensitize the commitmentphobic before he is compelled to act on his fears.

5. Refuse to assume responsibility and guilt for outrageous male behavior.

6. Make the sort of changes in your attitude that will produce the changes you want in his behavior.

7. Stop him before he runs again.

In the following chapters, you'll learn how.

Chapter 2

IS THE MAN YOU LOVE AFRAID TO LOVE YOU?

IDENTIFYING THE MAN WHO IS AFRAID OF COMMITMENT—THE PATTERN IN THE CONFUSION

If you know what to look for, it's easy to recognize the man who suffers from commitmentphobia. Caught between his need for love and his overwhelming fear, he is incapable of masking his conflict. Typically his confusion creates a readily discernible behavior pattern—fingerprints, so to speak.

When a commitmentphobic meets a woman he's attracted to, the intensity of his interest often seduces her into thinking that she has the upper hand in the relationship. At the beginning, he often makes her feel so secure that she tends to ignore the clues that give away his problem. Later, when she is already involved, his behavior may be so contradictory that she excuses or rationalizes his commitmentphobic symptoms; his scenarios are often so bizarre that it's hard to believe that the man who was once so adoring has become so weird.

The typical commitmentphobic is confused, and confusing. A woman who is involved with one will often describe him as being "like two different people." And he is. This is a man who is struggling with some very difficult demons. On the one hand, he has a tremendous desire to get involved in a relationship. On the other, whenever this happens, he is overwhelmed by his need to get away. That is his problem—until you become involved with him, and it becomes yours.

But however severe, or mild, his problem may be, trust me when I tell you that he doesn't really disguise his conflict about commitment. He may try to mask it. He may try to rationalize it, or explain it away. But he really can't control it. As a result, his internal conflict drives him to act in very specific ways. It's there if you want to see it. This chapter will show you how.

Women, unfortunately, have an equally predictable way of responding. When a woman gets involved with a commitment-phobic, it's very difficult for her to know exactly what's happening. His initial approach is often so romantic, it's the stuff that dreams are made of. If you are such a woman, detach yourself from your experiences with this man for just a moment—detach yourself from the painful memories, the frustration, the anger —and look at yourself and these other women from a third-person perspective.

I have spoken to many women at length, women who are, no doubt, very much like you. And believe me, I know these women are not stupid, nor are they gullible. They are bright, perceptive, sensible, and sensitive. Yet when each tells her story, it is stunningly clear that she has been manipulated by a man who can't love. From a comfortable distance, these men seem so transparent, their behavior so outrageous, their intent so obvious. Yet, when this is happening to you, when he is telling you how much he loves you, needs you, wants you, you want to believe him and you make every effort *to* believe him, even when you are skeptical.

So, in spite of all your reservations, your skepticism, your doubts, you let yourself be convinced and decide to give this man, and this love, a chance. Unfortunately, that's exactly when the trouble starts. But you can't blame yourself. Although you also behave predictably, *he* is the one with the problem. Your only fault is that you have been sociologically groomed to respond favorably to a man who acts like the knight in shining armor, the hero who is going to pull you up onto his horse and take you riding into the sunset.

So what can you do about it? I firmly believe that there are many things you can do about it. The first thing, and what this chapter is all about, is recognizing his pattern when you see it.

THE PURSUIT/PANIC SYNDROME IN ACTION: THE WARNING SIGNS OF COMMITMENTPHOBIA

All of the following women are talking about relationships with men who pursued and panicked. Each of these women is feeling unhappy and rejected, as well as confused about what is going on. Each of these relationships provides a good example of the way a man behaves when commitmentphobic anxiety is controlling his life:

"When he's with me, everything is wonderful. But he always runs away from it; sometimes I don't see or hear from him for weeks."

"Within hours of getting engaged, he changed. Now he's moody, withdrawn, and always looking to pick fights. I thought we would be so happy—I don't understand what happened."

"Alone in my apartment, you can't believe how close we are. But when we go anywhere, he almost acts like he doesn't know me. Even when we walk down the street, he always manages to walk faster than me, or slower, or different—anything so we are not moving at the same pace."

"He said he was lonely and acted like having a relationship with me was the most important thing in the world . . . When we started going out, he wasn't seeing anybody else, but within a couple of months he started dating two other women. I know he loves me, but it's making me crazy."

"He saw me walk out of my office building, and he decided he would return at the same time every day until I walked by again—just so he could meet me! He was so wonderful to me. Then after six months, he passed the bar exam, and he had a birthday—in the same week. I called some of his friends, and we gave him a surprise party. Two days later, with no explanations, he said he couldn't see me anymore."

"We met at work . . . he did everything he could to get my attention. Finally we went out. We talked and talked and talked. He cried when he told me how badly he felt about his divorce and his kids. Finally, at four in the morning, we wound up in my apartment. It felt so close it seemed silly and childish to say no, when I knew how much we both wanted each other. I thought we were starting a real relationship, and I just wanted to be honest. Now, at work, not only does he barely acknowledge me, he sounds angry if he has to say anything to me. I can't believe he rejected me just because I slept with him."

"It started the night before the wedding when he began to find fault with what I was wearing, saying it was inappropriate for a middle-aged bride. It was so cruel, I went into shock. He had been so kind until then, I just thought he was having last-minute jitters. Now, a year later, nothing I do or say pleases him . . . nothing. But when I suggest a divorce, he cries and promises to change."

HIS PATTERN IN LOVE—HOW HE AVOIDS "FOREVER AFTER"

If you have attracted the interest of a commitmentphobic, you will discover that the man changes drastically when a relationship runs the risk of going on "forever."

Typically, the classic commitmentphobic relationship goes through four separate and distinct stages.

1. The Beginning: All he can think about is how much he wants you.
2. The Middle: He knows he has you, and it scares him.
3. The End: You want him, and he's running scared.
4. The Bitter End: It's all over, and you don't know why.

THE BEGINNING: FEARLESS PURSUIT

This stage is typified by the hard sell. He is obviously taken by you, and is trying desperately to make you feel the same way. To accomplish this, he pulls out all the stops. How long the

Beginning lasts depends upon how long it takes him to make the sale and what he perceives as the commitment point of no return.

Typically:

1. He comes on strong and is probably more interested in you than you are in him.

2. Within a very short time, he indicates that he thinks you are "special" and seems to have few if any reservations about you or his decision to pursue you.

3. He has a rocky history with women, but he makes you think he will be different with you

4. He does everything he can to impress you: If he has money, he spends it; if he has special talents, he exhibits them; if he has "sensitivity" or "emotional depth," he reveals it.

5. He appears vulnerable and acts as if he needs the relationship more than you do.

6. He indicates, either with words or with deeds, that he is looking for a meaningful, monogamous relationship, not just a superficial affair.

7. He is willing to go way out of his way to be with you and do things for you, breaking other plans, traversing great distances if necessary, etc.

8. He phones all the time, often "just to say hello" or "just to hear your voice."

9. He openly engages in "future talk," making plans for things the two of you will do together. He may even refer to the two of you as "we."

10. He acts as though you're a priority in his life.

11. He appears sensitive to women's issues and puts down other men who are thoughtless and unkind to women.

12. He does everything he can to convince you to trust him—and eventually you do.

13. He convinces you to make a commitment (emotional and/ or sexual) to him.

THE MIDDLE: THE FIRST RUMBLINGS OF PANIC

The Middle usually starts when there is a definite shift of power in the relationship. Now *you* are "sold" on him, and he feels that some form of real commitment is expected from him. For the first time in the relationship, he must come face to face with his own commitment problem. This stage is typified by conflict and doubt. You are giving him what he said he wanted, but instead of being happy, he is feeling pressured and ambivalent. When he is with you, he is feeling the first anxiety-ridden pangs of commitmentphobia. Often he doesn't understand it, so he begins rationalizing his fear and looking for flaws in you. In some relationships, the man's panic is very intense; in this case this stage is very brief, and he immediately moves on to the End. In others, this stage drags on interminably, keeping the relationship alive for many miserable years.

Typically:

1. He seems to be backing away, as though something is scaring him. He may not call as often, be as attentive, etc.

2. Where his intentions were once clear, his words and actions are now full of mixed messages.

3. He makes it clear that certain important parts of his life, such as friends, family, or work, are "forbidden zones," and he excludes you from one or more of them. He often has seemingly plausible excuses for doing this.

4. He is wary of events that include your family and friends, and avoids spending any serious time with these people. It's as though he is sure that somebody there knows the truth about him, and it is not good.

5. He treats you as though you are less of a priority and has a million excuses why.

6. His sexual pattern changes, and he may subtly be turning you into the aggressor.

7. He establishes a definite schedule of when and how he has time for you—on his terms—and always seems to have other demands that have to be met first; by definition, this disturbs the natural flow of a relationship.

8. He treats most of your requests as though they are demands and seems to resent being "counted on." He indicates that he resents "expectations," though he doesn't make it clear what these expectations are.

9. He doesn't seem to "hear" what you are saying and seems to be paying less and less attention to your needs.

10. He praises you for being loyal, devoted, intelligent, a good cook, understanding—all "wife-like" qualities—but they simultaneously seem to make him uncomfortable.

11. He begins to find problems associated with seeing you. For example: He can "never find parking near your house." He has "trouble sleeping in your bed." You "live too far away." He is "allergic to your cat."

12. He starts to find fault with you and looks for reasons why the relationship will not work. He may hurt you by bringing these "faults" to your attention, particularly if they are things you can't change (e.g., "I'm not sure if my parents can ever accept the fact that you are one of the following: Irish, Italian, black, white, Jewish, Gentile, Wasp, short, tall, divorced, too old, too young, too rich, too poor, too medium). Or he may save them up and spring them on you when he finally decides the relationship should end. (Incidentally, these "faults" rarely have anything to do with anything you have done to him; they almost always have to do with the "way you are." He was fully aware of these qualities when he entered the relationship and persuaded you to join him.)

13. He may start leaving clues that he is looking at, thinking about, or actually seeing another woman. (Often it is a woman from his past.)

14. If he has been seeing another woman, he lies about it or plays it down, continuing to assure you that you are the most important person in his life.

15. He is obviously deeply conflicted, and may respond to your threats to end the relationship by promising to change; he may even cry.

16. Despite everything he says, nothing ever changes; he doesn't allow the relationship to grow or progress and he won't talk about it.

THE END: RUNNING SCARED

There is no better way to sum up this stage than to say that the commitmentphobic is "on the run." The man you knew at the beginning has disappeared: Your all-out Romeo has turned into the Artful Dodger. He got in too deep, and he knows it.

He may be conflicted about his emotions, but his strongest impulse is to get away. If it all started too fast, this stage can be reached within hours. There are, however, many men who would rather let the woman take responsibility for the break-up; they will usually drag on the End until you take action.

Typically:

1. His attitude toward you has almost totally changed, and he leaves obvious clues that he is on the way out.

2. He spends less time with you and doesn't bother to give you much of an explanation.

3. He inists upon flexibility and space.

4. He breaks dates and changes plans.

5. He is moody much of the time, but he still blames it on something else; he may go so far as to say, "It's not you."

6. He still confuses you by what he *says* and gives very mixed messages. One minute it's harsh rejection or fault-finding; the next it's sentimental love or total approval.

7. He withdraws sexually and blames it on work, fatigue, or illness. He implies that if you were really understanding, you would understand.

8. He won't do anything at all to try to improve the relationship—he won't even talk about it.

THE BITTER END: THE GREAT ESCAPE

In this stage, the commitmentphobic is trying to negotiate an ending, but he is rarely sure how to do it. Whenever it's possible, he will find a way to blame the woman or make her responsible. He may also vacillate. Why? Because his decision to leave relieves some of his anxiety, and he may once again start to have feelings for the woman. His confusion and inability to understand what he is experiencing often produces behavior that appears bizarre and makes the woman think he is undergoing some sort of breakdown. He typically ends the relationship in one or some combination of three possible ways. Here's how:

Typically:

1. He *provokes* you into ending it by starting a huge argument or engaging in particularly outrageous behavior.

2. He *withdraws* so totally (he may even move) that the relationship dies of attrition.

3. He stops calling, doesn't return your phone calls, and totally *disappears* from your life, often in a way that is bizarre as well as destructive.

CURTAIN CALLS: WHEN HE COMES BACK

Often all the commitmentphobic needs to relieve his anxiety is distance. The relationship is over, so he is no longer frightened. Thus, the feelings he has for you are free to surface in this non-threatening environment. No longer panicked by the trap, he misses you! So he calls. When that happens, usually the whole scenario is played out all over again. The only difference: This time it's faster.

Chapter 3

WHY HE CAN'T LOVE

WHAT IS THIS MAN AFRAID OF?

RUSS: Thirty-two-year-old investment banker—single.

Russ, who is about 6 feet 2 inches tall, looks more like a professional athlete than anything else. A thirty-two-year-old MBA, he's pulling down well over $100,000 a year. Russ would be making more, but he doesn't like to stay in one place too long and changes jobs, on average, at least once a year. Hence in most years, there is a period of unemployment.

Russ comes from a large close-knit family. His parents, his two older sisters, and his younger brother are all happily married. Although he has bought himself a summer house near a beach and a ski house in the mountains, he continues to live with his parents. He says he goes his own way and finds it both convenient and economical to continue to live at home.

Russ has had very few relationships that lasted longer than a few months. He says women usually start getting serious after about five or six dates, and he doesn't want it. When this happens, he withdraws, stops calling, and puts his home phone on a machine or doesn't answer. In the office, his secretary is told to say he isn't there.

He remembers liking and sleeping with at least half a dozen women who he pursued for a evening or two and then didn't call again. In his personal and social life, he "hates the formality of planning ahead." Business is "totally different," and he has no problems arranging meetings weeks in advance. He makes a clear distinction between business and personal affairs. "Decisions are easy for me to make" he says. "Commitments are almost impossible."

As far as women are concerned, Russ doesn't like the idea of knowing that he has a "permanent" commitment to anybody and says the only way he will be able to handle marriage is if he thinks of it as "temporary." He doesn't feel the same way about children, who "are not permanent," but are "only borrowed for about fourteen or fifteen years at best."

Last year Russ had what was probably the most important relationship of his life with a woman named Susan, who he met through work. It lasted a year. Russ says, "She ended it."

It began as most of Russ's involvements begin:

"I'm very aggressive in everything I do. Relationships are no different. With Susan, I started off very fast. The first night we went out, she admired a dress we noticed in a store window. I went out the next morning, bought the dress, and had it delivered to her office. I thought it was very romantic . . . and it worked. Within three or four weeks, we were living together in her apartment."

Although Russ moved into Susan's apartment, he makes it clear that he didn't consider that a commitment and has many explanations to justify his logic.

"Living together is just an arrangement; it's just convenient. It doesn't mean that there is a commitment on either side. As a matter of fact, it states very clearly that you're not sure; that's why you're not getting married. The other reason I had for living with her was that I have very limited time available. Living with her saved me commuting time, and she wouldn't have seen me as often if I had to drive back and forth. I made it clear we were both free to see other people."

Russ says everything was fine for the first few months, and everyone told him that he and Susan made the perfect couple. People just assumed they would be getting married.

"She did everything she could to please me. She was there

for me, constantly. *Constantly.* All I had to do was say I wanted to do something or go somewhere, and she was ready. At first it was fine, then I felt as though I was suffocating . . . suffocated.

"Look, it's the same old story. If you're looking for an excuse to find fault with someone, it's easy. I started to find fault with her. I was aggravated by her trying to change the ground rules, make it more serious than it was. When I get that way, I start having heart palpitations. I remember an incident where I went with her to go see her family. I didn't want to be there, and we had to stay through a whole family dinner, and I didn't want to stay. I just wanted to get out of there. I thought, 'What the hell am I doing here? This is too serious for me.' I had palpitations from it."

Russ says there were several contributing factors to the end of the relationship.

"I met this woman at the florist where I bought Susan flowers. I didn't think Susan would be home, so I took her back to the apartment with me. Susan came home early and found us together."

I asked Russ why he didn't drive with the woman to his beach house, a couple of hours away, or go with her to a hotel. He says he didn't know the woman that well, and it wasn't worth the trouble. It was obviously worth enough trouble to risk threatening his relationship with Susan. As one can imagine, Susan was very upset, but Russ convinced her that the woman was meaningless and that nothing like that would ever happen again. The relationship lasted another couple of months, but from that point forward, it was clearly in trouble.

"I guess I was afraid of making a permanent commitment to Susan, because the longer the relationship lasted, the more abusive I became. I was a real bastard to her. I didn't come home, I dumped a lot of office stress on her, I saw other women, I froze her out and stopped talking. She was attractive, she was bright. She was everything you could want, yet it wasn't enough. What finally happened is that one night Susan threatened me with somebody else. She said there was another man who said he wanted to be with her. She said he would spend more time with her, be nicer, et cetera. I don't take threats. I felt guilty because I think she really wanted me to stop her from seeing him, to say, 'No, don't do it.' I couldn't back down because if I backed down she'd have me totally wrapped around her finger, and if anything ever went wrong, she'd know how to threaten me. We woke up the next morning, and that was that. I packed a bag while she was taking a shower, and I left. Susan was too perceptive . . . it's great sometimes, but it's no fun fighting with yourself all day. She said I was too afraid to *ever* make a serious commitment, that I would never be able to really love anyone. The more I think about it, the more I think maybe she's right."

TOO FRIGHTENED TO LOVE

If you are involved with a commitmentphobic, the first thing you have to know is that it is what *he* is feeling, not what you are doing, that is filling him with terror and confusion; it is what *he* is thinking, not what you are saying, that is driving a wedge into the relationship. And it is *his* tortured, convoluted outlook on life, love, and relationships that is making him flee.

It's easy to say that men like Russ can't love because they are afraid of commitment. It's more difficult to understand why. A woman often knows when her man is running away from commitment, but that doesn't necessarily help her understand it or stop it. Nor does it help her protect herself from his destructive behavior.

Until now, most attempts to understand commitment anxiety have been approached only from the woman's perspective. Entire books, and the theories behind them, are based almost exclusively on women's experiences with commitmentphobics and their interpretations of these experiences. At the very best, this is exposing only half of the problem.

It's clear to me that there is painfully little insight available for women into the mind of the man who can't love. Without this insight, women, and some therapists, tend to examine only the woman's behavior when trying to understand why a relationship went on the rocks. Unfortunately, women also tend to blame themselves for their failures in love. They say things like, "I was too needy," or "I let it progress too fast," or "I guess I was stupid to trust him," or "I wonder how I failed him."

When the problems with this man start, most women tend to react in a similar fashion. Typically, the woman will assume that she can make the man feel better about being involved in a monogamous relationship, and thus his fears of commitment will dissolve. To make him "feel better," she may, for example, try to be warmer and more loving; she may cater to him in a dozen different ways in an effort to reinforce the fact that she cares and that she will not reject him. Other women try to make him feel better by ignoring his fears and hoping they will go away.

Unfortunately, all of these well-intentioned gestures tend to have the opposite effect on the man who is afraid. If you make light of the situation, it is interpreted as a "trick," while if you make an extra effort to be kind and loving, it is interpreted as an attempt to tighten the web of entrapment. Either way, all you've succeeded in doing is pushing him further away.

All too frequently, women bend themselves into pretzels trying to become more loving, more giving, more attractive, more sympathetic. But you will ultimately discover that the problem is not with your shortcomings or imperfections. Traditional self-improvement isn't going to work. You can dye your hair a dozen different colors, you can take a dozen different courses, you can change your weight, your friends, and your profession, you can reshape your body and your mind a thousand different ways— but his problem will remain. Why? Because the problem doesn't lie in the particulars. His reaction is not a reaction to you, it's a reaction to the act of making a commitment. And his fear of commitment will not be alleviated by making these kinds of changes. It can only be modified with a clear understanding of the depth and breadth of this man's fear.

You see, his fear is not a fear that will go away with time or with love. For this is not a man who is afraid of love, it is a man who is afraid of what love represents; this is not a man who is afraid of you, it is a man who is afraid of what you represent. Essentially this is a man who is afraid of one word, and that word is *FOREVER*.

FOREVER IS A LONG, LONG TIME

The fear of commitment can provoke a variety of unpleasant symptoms, the predominant one being anxiety. If a man is mildly commitmentphobic, his relationships may elicit nothing more than a vague sense of unease. This mild anxiety reaction can be alleviated simply by distancing himself emotionally. But if his fear is intense, his anxiety reaction will be severe, and the prospect of "hand in hand forever" may strike genuine terror in his heart and soul.

WHAT IS IT ABOUT COMMITMENT AND "FOREVER" THAT'S SO FRIGHTENING?

In the past few years, men's flight from commitment has reached epidemic proportions. A plethora of books and magazine articles have been written speculating why. Some, for example, suggest that men's inability to commit is a backlash against years of being trapped in the repressive role of breadwinner. Others believe that it is at least partially attributable to men's fear of the strong, independent "new woman"—especially if the man has had a history of feeling inferior, unworthy, or rejected. Many assert that men's inability to commit is merely a reflection of immaturity—a refusal to "grow up" and accept responsibility. Most recently, it has been suggested that this is all a product of the Playboy mentality—the belief that one should not make any permanent commitments as long as one can keep "trading up" to a better, more fantasy-like companion.

There are, of course, the more traditional explanations as well: Oedipal conflicts, prostitute/madonna conflicts, fear of rejection, selfishness, narcissism, low self-esteem, etc. But while all of these factors may indeed contribute to, aggravate, or help shape the problem, *none* can account for the many ramifications of commitmentphobia—ramifications, as we'll see, that extend far beyond the realm of relationships. In other words, while all of these factors may somehow *affect* the problem, none, either alone or in combination, actually *determine* the problem.

So what *is* so frightening about commitment? My first clue came to me while working on an entirely different project. As fate would have it, last year a prominent psychiatrist asked me to work with him in the completion of a controversial new book on the nature and origins of phobias.

This project proved to be a blessing in disguise. As I interviewed patients for the phobia book, they often asked me what else I was writing. Frequently this would lead to discussions about the fear of commitment, a subject most of these patients were all too happy to talk about. As a result, these "double interviews" provided me with a whole new pool of subjects— and what a special pool it was.

I will never forget the reaction I got from one of the first phobic patients I told about my book. "Commitments!" he exclaimed. "I don't have any problems with commitments. I don't make any." He then proceeded to launch into a forty-five-minute dissertation on how the fear of commitment had ruled and ruined his life. Although it didn't mean anything to me at the time, this man was being treated by the doctor for severe claustrophobia.

Frighteningly similar conversations were to follow with many of the phobic patients, but not all. For with little exception, it was the *claustrophobics* who always seemed to be most troubled by commitment. And it was the *claustrophobics* who had the greatest difficulty forming and maintaining monogamous relationships, regardless of how badly they seemed to want and need love.

COMMITMENTPHOBIA: THE CLAUSTROPHOBIC CONNECTION

The dictionary defines *claustrophobia* as an abnormal fear of small enclosed spaces. To the claustrophobic, the fear of being stuck or trapped within such a space provokes anxiety, dread, and often outright panic. Everyone acknowledges that some people are afraid of physically confining conditions, but many of the phobic patients I was interviewing were telling me that the very same type of fear and anxiety response could be provoked by *symbolic* representations of being trapped, stuck, or held down. These symbolic representations included jobs, lifestyles, and relationships.

Obviously there was a connection. Yet I was slow to see just what that connection was. But as I spoke to more and more patients, many pieces of this confusing puzzle began to fit neatly into place. Claustrophobia and commitmentphobia . . . were we really dealing with one and the same thing? Was commitment-phobia nothing more than one of the many ramifications of claus-trophobic anxiety? Were men's commitment problems merely a psychological, "symbolic" extension of their claustrophobic fear of being physically stuck or trapped?

This certainly made perfect sense. Commitments were per-manent. To honor a commitment was to be bound to that de-cision, to that thing, or to that person . . . *forever*. What could be more confining? What could be more claustrophobic?

Then I thought about the many "normal" nonphobic men I had interviewed. Their fears of commitment were no different than those of the phobic patients, yet they rarely mentioned anything about being claustrophobic or feeling claustrophobic in their relationships. Instead, most seemed quite certain that their relationship failures had usually been the woman's fault. Were all of these men just rationalizing? Were they all really "closet claustrophobics"? Were, perhaps, the claustrophobic pa-tients who had sought a doctor's help merely more in touch with their fear? I supposed that to some extent this was true. But what I really suspected was that an important piece of the puzzle was still missing.

Excited by my discovery, but still somewhat frustrated by its lack of completeness, I decided to bring this problem to the attention of the psychiatrist I was working for. He was quick to point out the importance of recognizing the widespread existence of claustrophobic *tendencies* in the majority of the human pop-ulation, as well as in many other animal species. Lock twenty human beings—or mice for that matter—in a tiny room and, given enough time, the vast majority will become uncomfortable, anxious, aggressive, or even downright panic-stricken. (Such studies have often been done with laboratory animals.) Under normal circumstances, most of these individuals wouldn't show any claustrophobic characteristics. But if the environment is sufficiently limiting, these tendencies can be triggered and brought to the surface in virtually *anyone*.

A CLOSER LOOK AT WHAT COMMITMENTS MEAN

Now let's take a look at the nature of commitments. A commitment, by definition, is the act of binding or obligating oneself to something or someone, be it a job, a car, a pet, or a woman. Once committed, you are "stuck" with that obligation for the duration of the commitment.

It is easy to see how the act of committing can provoke severe claustrophobic anxiety. If a commitment is long-term, and a man intends to honor that commitment, it can feel as restrictive as being locked inside a small room. If the commitment is forever, as marriage is supposed to be, it can feel like being locked inside a closet. Though the man is not being *physically* restricted, he feels *psychologically* restricted, and the sensations are frighteningly similar.

In other words, psychological confinement can be just as claustrophobic as physical confinement, with both representing a loss of freedom. As a result, any serious or lengthy commitment becomes viewed as a trap, and, like any other trap, it triggers anxiety. The greater the trap, the greater the anxiety and the greater the urge to flee.

What is clear to me now is that men's reactions to the claustrophobic restrictiveness of commitment are no different than any other phobic reactions. In other words, commitmentphobia is not just a clever eighties catch phrase. *Commitmentphobia is a true phobia*, replete with all of the classic physical and psychological phobic symptomatology. What is also clear is that if you truly wish to understand and change the commitmentphobic's destructive behavior pattern, you have to understand what is shaping that pattern—i.e., the phobia itself. But to do that, it would help first to know a little bit more about phobias in general.

THE PHOBIC RESPONSE: AN INTERNAL ALARM

When a person senses some type of threat or danger, the body has a very specific way of reacting. This reflexive response—

this automatic, unconscious "alarm system"—is characterized by one or more of the following symptoms:

Waves of anxiety
A sense of dread
Hyperventilating and/or labored breathing
Suffocating sensations
A skipping or racing heart
Stomach distress
Excessive sweating
Sweating or chills ("cold feet")

In many situations this response is entirely appropriate and expected. It is not surprising, for example, to experience these symptoms when confronted by a snarling Doberman or an armed assailant. But often these very same symptoms are triggered by a far more subtle threat, even a seemingly innocuous object or circumstance—such as an elevator, a bridge, a spider, or a relationship. When we have an inappropriate reaction such as this, when the body's fear response seems greatly exaggerated or totally irrational, we call it a phobic response.

Thanks to the work of various noted stress researchers, we know that this internal alarm is not an all-or-nothing response. On the contrary, the intensity of these symptoms can vary considerably, depending on the sensitivity of the individual and the intensity of the perceived threat.

A one-alarm response, for example, may be nothing more than a slightly elevated breathing rate, increased perspiration, and a modest release of anxiety. Subjectively, this entire one-alarm response would probably feel like nothing more than common everyday anxiety.

A two- or three-alarm response, in contrast, might be characterized by substantial but seemingly manageable anxiety, further elevation in heartbeat and respiratory rate, stomach distress, and considerable tension. These symptoms will make you feel uncomfortable in your surroundings. They may even provoke mild fear, panicky feelings, and a desire to get away from or avoid whatever it is that seems to be making you so anxious, be it a tunnel, a snake, or your lover.

If the internal alarm is producing a four- or five-alarm response, the symptoms will be quite strong. You may be flooded with anxiety or overwhelmed by a variety of other magnified symptoms. Collectively, all of this is experienced as fear, if not outright panic, and it will compel you to avoid or escape from whatever seems to be triggering these frightening symptoms.

Because the phobic response can vary, men's behavior can also vary. Some men are terrified of *all* commitments, and act accordingly. Others can handle short-term commitments, but panic over anything long-term or permanent. Still others are capable of making all types of commitments, but are never truly at ease once these commitments have been made (otherwise known as chronic anxiety). In other words, to a large extent, the variety of phobic responses accounts for the variety of commitmentphobic types and the variety of commitmentphobic reactions.

WHAT ABOUT LOVE?

For a woman, the most painful part of this experience is that the man's attitude seems to change so drastically. As far as she is concerned, *love*, not fear, is the issue. She is probably idealistic as well as romantic. She is the product of a culture that told her that love could conquer all. She thought she was involved in a love affair. Was the man lying by word or deed? How could anyone lose interest or fall out of love so quickly? What happened? Did she do something wrong? The transformation from what appears to be an ardent, involved, and concerned lover and friend to a man who seems detached, conflict-ridden, and disinterested is, at best, confusing. The change is often so drastic it is little wonder that the woman worries that she might have done something to precipitate his behavior.

If you are that woman, it is important to be aware that this man can forget that he cares about you. He can forget how much he enjoys himself with you. He can even forget about terrific sex. He may want to consider your feelings, but his discomfort and confusion are too great. Yet even if he could stop running long enough to consider your feelings, and even if he was overwhelmed with guilt, it still wouldn't change his direction. In fact, it usually has the reverse effect: The guiltier he feels, the more he feels trapped and the more he wants to get away.

If you are a woman who has tried to relate to a commitmentphobic, his behavior probably seems totally inexplicable. Who can understand such strangeness? But it really isn't that confusing once you understand that the reason he runs has nothing to do with liking you, being attracted to you, or enjoying himself with you. He runs away because he is aware that the relationship cannot continue without his making some form of real commitment—and this is something that he simply cannot do.

When you keep this in mind, it is easier to understand why he has a real problem negotiating an honest relationship. He knows that he hasn't given it his best shot. He also knows that he has probably been the initiator and pursuer. If it is a relationship of any duration, he has probably told you more than once that he loves you. Until the final moments, he has probably continued to act as though he wanted to be in the relationship. But the time has come where he either goes forward or gets out, and he can't go forward. He isn't naive enough to think that you might understand what he is feeling. Besides, if you did, he might have to work things out. And then he might actually have to make a commitment. But that's not possible—after all, that's what scared him in the first place.

COMMITMENTPHOBIA: A TRUE PHOBIA?

If, as I have asserted, the man who can't love suffers from commitmentphobia, and if commitmentphobia is a *true* phobia, then one would expect the commitmentphobic man to experience many or all of the classic phobic symptoms, at least to some degree, when he is confronted by the phobic trigger (i.e., commitment). In order to investigate this possibility, I asked all of the men I interviewed the following questions: Have any of your close relationships ever triggered uncomfortable physical symptoms such as stomachaches, palpitations, or hyperventilation?

When would this happen? Did you ever feel smothered, choked, or suffocated by a close relationship? Do you recall when this would happen? Has a close relationship ever triggered any feelings akin to panic? Were you having problems at the time, or was everything going well?

The answers were nothing less than fascinating. Not only did they consistently confirm my hypothesis, but they clearly illustrated just how deeply and strongly the fear of commitment is felt. Throughout this book you will come across many men's answers to these questions, but the following typical examples should whet your appetite:

Joshua M. talking about his marriage:
"Now I know what it's like being a caged animal. Your freedom's taken away. You have nothing to live for."

Andy B. on his feelings about his ex-fiancée:
"I'd see her and I'd freeze . . . go back around the corner and head in the opposite direction. I'd feel a swell of blood and adrenaline hitting my head, saying, 'Get out of here . . . run . . . escape! This big fat pillowcase is coming down over your head . . . Escape!' "

Gregory D. on women in general:
"Whenever a woman thinks too highly of me, I feel trapped by her expectations of me—the expectation of always having to be there—and then I want to get away from her and those feelings."

Frank M. on relationships:
"When I feel like I'm getting trapped, I react violently. I get smothered . . . then I get crazy . . . the hair on the back of my neck stands up."

Dick D. on why he ended his last relationship:
"We were in a room full of people. I was sitting in a chair, and she was sitting on the floor next to me with her hands around my feet. I looked down and felt like I was in chains."

A FEAR THAT PERMEATES THE SOUL

Most phobia experts have noted the extent to which phobics are obsessed, overwhelmed, and controlled by their fears. These fears are such an integral part of the phobic's life that their presence is felt not only while the phobic is awake, but often while he is asleep as well. It is not uncommon, for example, for someone with a fear of heights to have "falling" nightmares or for someone with a fear of water to have nightmares about drowning. Now that we have established the true phobic qualities of commitmentphobia it should come as no surprise that many commitmentphobics have commitment nightmares, especially at the time they are involved in a relationship in which "forever" or "commitment" are real possibilities.

TOM'S STORY

To understand what it is about "commitment" and "forever" that frightens these men so, it is important to hear how *men* experience the problem. Consider, for example, my friend Tom. I've known Tom, a thirty-three-year-old systems analyst, for many years. Two years ago, both of Tom's sisters got married within months of each other. This precipitated several family discussions as to when he, the oldest child, would do likewise. Right around the same time, Tom started a new job. That's how he met Gloria. Gloria was Tom's supervisor, something he found especially provocative. This is how Tom recalls their relationship:

"Within hours of meeting Gloria I was smitten. She wasn't. I pushed, she was cool. I pushed some more. All day long I would sit and think about clever little lines to say to her, funny little notes to send her. Anything to get her attention and win her approval, without, of course, seeming like a total ass. She ran and I chased. She said we were too different. I assured her that this was not the case. It took time, four months to be exact, but one night, after a wonderful dinner in a romantic Italian restaurant, I convinced her to come back to my apartment and the affair began. I don't think I will ever forget how I felt after driving her home that first night. It wasn't what we had done. It was something she said that made me want to run. She said, 'I can't believe how lucky I am that I met you and that you managed to convince me that my hesitations were foolish.' She added, 'I'm glad you proved that my first impressions were wrong.'

"I suddenly realized that everything I had done had been far more effective than I could have imagined. Everything worked far too well. It had come too far too fast. Suddenly I was the one who wasn't ready, and I panicked. I found myself thinking things like, 'Don't do this . . . there are so many other women out there.'

"I had told her that I would call her the next day—a Saturday—but whenever I reached for the phone I would get a sinking feeling in the pit of my stomach. I was actually afraid to make the phone call, though I didn't quite know why.

"Then that night I had a dream, or more accurately, a nightmare. People laugh when I tell them this dream, but to me it was very real, very frightening, and not at all funny. I dreamt that I was at my own wedding. The room was huge and foreboding, with giant doors made of steel. No sooner did the dream begin than I found myself taking vows. When it was my turn to say, 'I do,' I was overcome by panic and dread. I wanted to run out but I couldn't because I'd allowed it to go too far. I had no choice so I said, 'I do.'

"The second those words were out of my mouth I felt sick. I thought, 'How could I have done this? My life is over.' The fear was so real and so profound that it startled me out of my sleep. When I woke I still felt the terror, but I was also angry at the woman in the dream for making me experience these awful feelings.

"I've had this dream many times since, but the first time was after that night with Gloria. At the time, I didn't really connect the dream to her. After all, the woman I had married in the dream wasn't Gloria. But somehow on Sunday my fear of phoning Gloria was even greater than it had been on Saturday. I also began resenting her for having the expectation that I would call.

"When I ran into her at work on Monday I was nervous and afraid. I told myself that I didn't want to confront any anger she might be harboring because I hadn't called. I told myself that she would argue with me, so I did everything I could to avoid talking to her, remaining distant and only semi-friendly. How could I explain to her what I was feeling? I could hardly understand it myself. All that I knew was that I wanted to get as far away from her as I possibly could. I realize that this was not my finest hour."

WHEN THERE'S NOWHERE TO GO BUT COMMITMENT

Tom's discomfort is not unusual. When the symptoms of commitmentphobia first surface, the man is often genuinely confused. After all, these reactions are not happening in a vacuum; somewhere there is a woman he genuinely cares about. But where the relationship had once produced feelings of pleasure, it is now evoking dread. Consequently, the man is torn. On the one hand, he has tender emotions toward the woman; on the other, he is experiencing anxiety, fear, and panic—feelings that make him want to back away.

Tom genuinely liked Gloria, and he was definitely attracted to her. When he described her to me, he stressed how competent, intelligent, and admirable she was as a human being. Yet, as he readily acknowledges, he treated her very badly. What was Gloria feeling? We don't know because Tom didn't give her a chance to tell him. But if she was anything like the women I've spoken to, she probably couldn't comprehend why a man who had spent months showering her with compliments slept with her just once, and then barely acknowledged her existence.

Tom told me he didn't think about Gloria's feelings at all. It didn't even occur to him that she might think something about her had turned him off—which was, of course, not the case. The fact is that the relationship had nowhere to go except toward commitment, and this set off Tom's internal alarm system. After that, all he could think about was putting out the fire.

WHEN PANIC SETS IN

Some men are chronically commitment-anxious. Others, like my friend Tom, are fine as long as they are pursuing a reluctant woman. But the moment she starts responding, everything changes. Instead of being the pursuer, he reacts as though he is being pursued. This reaction often has nothing to do with reality; the woman may be doing nothing more than giving him the response he seems to want. But his anxiety mechanism is reacting as though his life is being threatened.

By avoiding the relationship, not dealing with the woman, and, ultimately, running away, the commitmentphobic is able to alleviate his anxiety. He may feel guilty, but this is not nearly as frightening or painful as the commitment anxiety. To this confused, anxiety-ridden man, the solution is simple: If taking charge of his life is a top priority, he has to back away from the relationship, and, consequently, the woman.

A FIGHT OR FLIGHT RESPONSE

The phobic anxiety response is commonly referred to as the "fight or flight" response. This reflexive reaction to danger is present not only in humans, but in most other higher animals as well. The role of the fight or flight response in animal survival, including the survival of human animal, is clear. It is nature's way of mobilizing our defense systems and preparing us for a confrontation with danger. When operating properly, it is a vital mechanism that insures the preservation of the species by preparing us to fight the source of the threat, or to take flight. Unfortunately, when it is not operating properly, as in the case of extreme phobic behavior, it can be terribly destructive.

The irony of the fight or flight label is not lost on any woman who has lived through the trials and tribulations of being involved with a commitmentphobic man. For once this man feels threatened by the commitment "trap," once his body has mobilized, he has two choices: flee from commitment, or stay and fight it by fighting with you. Some men, of course, do a little bit of both, but whatever his choice, the relationship is ultimately left in ruins.

Why do some men flee while others attack? I suspect it depends on two things: the sensitivity of a particular individual's alarm system and the way he views the sanctity of the relationship "contract." But what is all too clear is that both of these behavior patterns—fighting and taking flight—are the result of the same underlying phobic response.

LEAVING JUST WHEN THE GOING GETS GOOD

What is perhaps most fascinating about the commitmentphobic is that he rarely runs or fights when the relationship is *bad*; he runs or fights when it is *good*. This seems to completely contradict common sense. A bad relationship is something to fight over or run from, a good relationship is something to value and cherish—right? Not for the commitmentphobic. His actions are not governed by common sense, they are governed by his exaggerated fear of commitment. Therefore, when the relationship becomes truly close and intimate, he feels more trapped because he knows he has no excuses for leaving. As long as the relationship is troubled, he knows he has an excuse for leaving, and there is no threat of entrapment. Therefore, typically, when the relationship is going well, the alarm is tripped. When this happens, commitment anxiety comes rushing to the surface and, before you know it, he is fighting or fleeing. An example many women have given me is the man who leaves or picks a fight after a particularly good weekend or right after the woman has done something especially loving or supportive. This seemingly inexplicable behavior leaves a woman no choice but to conclude: I am involved with a man who cannot love.

MISOGYNIST OR COMMITMENTPHOBIC?

It is interesting and important to note that in the past, the man who stays and fights has often been labeled a misogynist— a man who hates women. But once you understand the dynamics of the commitmentphobic response, it is suddenly clear that this label is totally inappropriate. This is not a man who hates women, this is a man who wishes he could love women. But he is a victim of his fear—a fear that gives him only two choices: leave or fight.

The commitmentphobic response also explains why so many of these men can be so warm and loving one moment and so abusive the next. If they truly hated women, they would be abusive all of the time. But this is simply not the case for the man who can't love. He can be extremely warm and loving—often to the point of excess—until he reaches his personal phobic threshold. Only then, when his internal alarm is suddenly tripped, does his rage come rushing to the surface. Although I am not asking you to pity this man, I am asking you to recognize that his personal demons make him a truly pathetic character—a man who is a prisoner of his own fear.

AN OLD PROBLEM WITH A NEW TWIST

Commitmentphobia is nothing new. Men have always been wary of commitment, and their knee-jerk response to closeness and entrapment is probably as old as the species itself. But today there is a difference. Today, unlike any other period in our history, the fear of commitment is destroying the fabric of our society.

What is both interesting and sad is that this sudden change is clearly attributable to the Sexual Revolution, the Women's Liberation Movement, consciousness-raising, and other important components that brought us to the "new equality." In other words, the very changes that helped to bring men and women closer together are simultaneously tearing them apart.

Back in the "good old days" it was bad form for a young man to remain single for too long. With some exceptions, the bachelor's lifestyle was not a coveted one. On the contrary, it was one that drew suspicious glances from nosy neighbors who quietly whispered among themselves, speculating about homosexual tendencies, sexual problems, and Oedipal conflicts.

But even if a man paid no attention to the neighbors, he still had to face the fact that the man who didn't marry always seemed to wind up becoming the caricatured pale-faced elderly son stuck at home, forever doting on his senile mother. Hardly an appealing fate. Besides, "getting involved" did not seem like such a big deal. The distancing courtship rituals of yesteryear were not anywhere near as emotionally or sexually threatening as they are today. If anything, it was the opposite. And let's face it, if one didn't wish to remain celibate for the duration of one's life, there were few avenues of opportunity open other than that of marriage. Therefore, the louder the body screamed for fulfillment, the more one found oneself being propelled down the only legitimate road that would silence those screams.

Even in the late 1950s marriage was still the only "sanctioned" life path for the average man. In *Hearts of Men*, noted feminist Barbara Ehrenreich reminds us that:

"The average age of marriage for men in the late fifties was twenty-three, and according to popular wisdom, if a man held out much longer, say even to twenty-seven, 'you had to wonder.' By the 1950's and 60's psychiatry had developed a massive weight of theory establishing that marriage—and within that, the breadwinner role—was the only normal state for the adult male. Outside lay only a range of diagnoses, all unflattering."

So, our prehistoric (pre-1960s) man allowed himself to be drawn into a monogamous relationship, made his commitments, and doused the fire burning in his soul. By the time he began to perceive the "walls closing in" around him, he was usually too far along in the commitment process to back away (especially if he thought her father was behind him).

The concept of the reluctant groom is hardly a myth. I suspect that the majority were reluctant, if not downright terrified. But once committed, there were few avenues of escape short of leaving town or joining the foreign legion. Society said he had to get married, so he got married.

Once married, the commitmentphobic was genuinely stuck, since divorce was neither accessible nor acceptable. If the urge to flee became too strong, which it often did, he was left with little choice but to do so within the confines of his marriage. Some men found alcohol to be an acceptable means of escape. Others immersed themselves in their work. Those who could get away with it had affairs, while others simply buried themselves in the daily newspaper and "tuned out" their wives. Many men, of course, did all of the above.

While many women may still be living through this kind of hell, today's relationships with commitmentphobics tend to be governed by a whole new set of dynamics. Thanks to the liberating influence of recent social changes, including the Women's Liberation Movement, the Sexual Revolution, and general consciousness-raising, men don't *have* to get married to obtain the love and sex that only marriage used to bring. And a single man can remain single well into his declining years (his forties, for sure) without raising more than a handful of eyebrows.

We call this progress, and it is. It is wonderful to be living during a time of such tremendous personal freedom, when such opportunities for fulfillment exist. But this freedom is wreaking havoc on our interpersonal relationships. Metaphorically speaking, men have been let out of the cage. And regardless of how warm and loving that environment could be, to the man it is still a cage. So, like any other animal who sees a cage, his first instinct is to run.

THE MANY RAMIFICATIONS OF COMMITMENTPHOBIA

As I discovered in the course of my interviews, commit-mentphobia is rarely restricted to interpersonal relationships. The commitmentphobic tends to fear commitment *in any way, shape or form*; he fears any thing or situation that has a fixed, permanent quality. His problems with women are only one part, though a significant one, of a much larger problem.

Tom, one of the first men I interviewed, pointed out that his fear of commitment was all-encompassing. He was so tuned in to his anxieties that his comments highlighted many things I was not, at that time, aware of. He pointed out that he tended to live the life of a vagabond because he could never fully commit himself to one place or one job. He rented a television set because he could never settle on just which set to buy, and noted that most major purchases were difficult or impossible to deal with.

Immediately suspecting that Tom's reactions were not unique, I began broadening my interviews to include questions concerning other, *seemingly* unrelated commitment problems. All of my in-depth interviews with men included the following questions: Do you have difficulty making major purchases? Do you own your home or pay rent? How long do you see yourself living there? Do you have a career that makes you happy? Do you have pets? Do you own a car? Do you have difficulty making long-range plans? Do you have difficulty making decisions in general? Do you have any other commitment-related quirks?

The answers to these questions were both fascinating and frightening. For the vast majority of interviewees, problems with personal relationships were just the tip of the commitment iceberg. The fear of commitment permeated these men's lives. For some, even the mention of the word commitment was enough to provoke considerable anxiety.

Some admitted that they were obsessed with commitment . . . haunted by it . . . often paralyzed by it. They also had commitment-related quirks I could never have dreamed of. Most didn't like to be committed to social engagements and were outrageously unreliable. Most hated the idea of committing themselves to serve on a committee. Several were reluctant to register to vote because they didn't want to commit to a party, or even to independent status. Some wouldn't write letters because they couldn't bear the thought of committing their thoughts to paper "forever." Many wouldn't talk into a tape recorder or make any other type of "permanent" recording. Several didn't like to write in ink. One wrote only in pencil and then erased everything he wrote. Two were aware of and brought up the fact that they were reluctant to put their names on their home mailbox.

It became all too clear. Commitmentphobia was not just a problem men had with women, it was a way of life. And these men didn't hate or fear women—just as they didn't hate or fear their careers or their homes. What they hated and feared was commitment itself, regardless of to whom or to what that commitment was being made. Let's take a closer look at some of the most common commitmentphobic behavior patterns.

A History of Unavailability and Inaccessibility That Extends Far Beyond the Way He Is with You

The vast majority of the men interviewed advertised their fears of being pinned down or their inaccessibility in one or more of the following ways:

1. Truly peculiar phone behavior.

The women told me, and the men confirmed, that they were

difficult to reach or find by phone, and that they were often unpredictable about returning phone calls. Some men purposely had no answering machines at home. Others had machines that were never turned on. The worst-case commitmentphobics either unplugged their phones or left them permanently attached to answering services or machines and made it clear to all their friends that they couldn't be depended on to return calls promptly.

More than one man had a secretary or an equivalent who was trained to give false information as to his whereabouts.

Other phone scenarios:

■ The fur salesman who encourages women to call him, gives specific instructions as to how and when to do so, and then is never at the number given.

■ The upper-echelon executive who gives out only one number: his local bar, where they are trained to say, "He hasn't been in yet."

■ The lawyer who changes his unlisted phone number to a new unlisted phone number every few months.

■ The copywriter who has an answering machine message that says: "You cannot reach me, and this machine does not take messages."

2. He is either reluctant to commit himself to plans with others or less than 100% reliable about carrying them out.

To a man, every major commitmentphobic I spoke to told me that he preferred not to commit himself to planning ahead in his personal life and didn't do so except when necessary. (Most resented that there was little flexibility with new women and that they were expected to make and keep dates.)

Many men admitted that they were unreliable with everyone in their personal lives, including family and friends. This was not true in work-related situations.

Mary, a nurse I interviewed, said in retrospect that if she had paid more attention to the way her ex-boyfriend Gordon treated his family and friends, she would never have gotten involved with him, let alone expected him to marry her.

"Gordon actually liked his mother and father, but he was awful to them. He never went to visit them because they lived three hours away and he had to think about it in advance, which he didn't want to do. They would come to visit him every couple of months, and then he resented the fact that he had to commit himself ahead to being available when they arrived. I know it upset his mother, but he didn't think it was odd that he should be so peculiar. He also refused to commit himself for any family function whatsoever, including holidays, weddings, and birthdays. Other than that, he had a good relationship with his parents, spoke to them on the phone regularly, and spoke about them and his childhood warmly. His parents were already in their seventies and he couldn't seem to realize that his attitude was placing a hardship on them."

Margo, an administrative assistant, has a similar story about her ex-boyfriend, Matt.

"When I first met Matt, who went on to break my heart and my bankbook because of all the money I spent on therapy trying to recover from my broken heart, one of the first things he told me was that his mother was angry at him. It seems he had promised to take her to a family wedding that was important to her, and he had overslept. He said it was not the first time something like this had happened, and he seemed genuinely upset about it. At the time, I chose to shore up his ego and his rationalizations by agreeing that his mother was difficult and demanding and that he was being self-protective by avoiding her. Later, I met a few of his friends; in the course of telling a story, one of them commented on how unreliable Matt was and how he rarely showed up as planned. Again I chose to ignore it, thinking that he probably had good reason to do this. At the end of our relationship, when he forgot, or slept through, or avoided at least half a dozen dates or events we had planned together, I remembered these stories."

3. **When he is in a social situation he doesn't enjoy, he often feels trapped. He seems to suffer more discomfort than most people and may appear sullen and moody.**

Every now and then, everyone feels trapped by a social situation—a party we don't want to attend, a concert we don't want to hear, a family event we would rather avoid. It's normal to feel some level of discomfort. It's also normal to realize that it will soon be over and that, for one reason or another, we have a social obligation to the situation or to a person. When this happens, we tell ourselves to take it in stride and try to make the most of it. Not so the typical commitmentphobic. He reacts vehemently. His cry of distress is so acute that one can only understand it when one realizes that he truly feels "stuck." His discomfort is so great that he cannot make the most of the situation, and he can make everyone, particularly the woman with him, miserable with his moodiness.

4. He may have work-related commitmentphobia.

Now let's look at the commitmentphobic's job pattern. Basically, he can't bear to feel trapped there either. Therefore, for the commitmentphobic to be happy with his work, it must meet at least one of the following criteria.

NOT STRUCTURED: A good example of this is any self-employed person who sets his own schedule and his own priorities.

NONPERMANENT: A commitmentphobic may be able to deal with a job that is both structured and confining, but only if he feels that the job does not define him or that it is not permanent.

For some commitmentphobics, their anxiety provokes even more extreme behavior. These men may never be able to settle into one job or one career and may constantly move from job to job or city to city.

Commitmentphobics tend to resist being defined by a job or a career, even when they are successful. An example of this is the lawyer/writer who teaches and plays in a jazz band weekends.

The bottom line is that they always want to feel that the possibility exists that they can get out from any job situation, should they want to. Some want to fairly often.

5. Many, if not all of the men, had living situations that were slightly off beat. For example:

■ He may have a permanently temporary attitude toward home base; this can be reflected by sublets or temporary leases, or by a serious reluctance to commit himself to buying furniture. Everything about his living situation is temporary or makeshift.

■ He may have an apartment with a real lease, but he rarely stays there, preferring to sleep at the homes of friends, ex-wives, girlfriends, etc.

■ His home totally reflects his attitude toward commitment. It is quite comfortable for him, but you can't help but get the feeling that his "lair" says, "I want to be alone." (An example of this is the forty-six-year-old advertising executive with a very comfortable apartment and a single bed. Or the thirty-eight-year-old computer programmer with a bathroom no woman would ever dream of using.)

■ His home is comfortable, but it was decorated or influenced by an ex-girlfriend or wife and is maintained almost as a shrine to that old relationship. In many cases, the woman was the rejected party, but this is not always evident by the decor or the way the commitmentphobic describes it and her.

■ He has a peculiar living arrangement that doesn't allow him to have women over; he may complain about it, but he doesn't change it.

6. Making major purchases is often traumatic.

Many commitmentphobics shop for VCRs in much the same way that they hunt for the perfect woman: they avoid committing themselves to major purchases and often regret the ones they make.

I talked to men who told me that buying a car was like making a decision to marry. "Once you've brought it home, you are 'stuck' with it, committed for a very long time," said one. Although the moment of purchase can be exhilarating, the reality of the decision may bring on anxiety, doubt, and self-flagellation.

Incidentally, although this particular phenomenon did not surprise me, it's not something I went searching for. But the first few men I interviewed all made a point of mentioning this particular aspect of their commitmentphobic anxiety.

In many cases, the men were more consciously aware of their anxieties surrounding making a purchasing commitment than they were of their anxieties about relationships. If you think about it, this isn't so difficult to understand. For example, it is clearly apparent to a man who can't buy a VCR that his choices are limited to what's on the market. If he can't make a commitment to buy one, it's obviously his problem. When he can't make a commitment to a woman, however, it's easy to rationalize with the all-too-familiar excuse, "I just haven't found the right one."

CAN WOMEN BE COMMITMENTPHOBIC?

As we come to the end of this chapter, it seems only fair that this one last issue is addressed. Once you understand the origins of commitmentphobia, it would seem only logical that this should not be a gender-specific problem. After all, women must certainly be susceptible to these same claustrophobic feelings that "forever" provokes. Wouldn't these women be as sensitive to commitment as men, equally frightened by the prospect of entrapment?

The answer to this is both yes and no. Yes, many women are scared of—even terrified by—commitment. Yet this hypersensitivity does not necessarily stop them from committing, at least not nearly to the extent that it stops men. Why? Because even though a woman may fear commitment, she has many other fears, needs, and instincts that are continually urging her to commit.

The most powerful force driving a woman to commit has to be her maternal instincts—her biological need to couple and reproduce. The survival of the species depends entirely on the continuation of the species, a task that Mother Nature has relegated primarily to women (a wise choice, no doubt). With few exceptions, all other fears and desires pale in the face of this most potent biological force. Hence, even if a woman is truly terrified of commitment in any way, shape, or form, the pull of her maternal instincts almost always manages to overwhelm these fears and anxieties . . . at least temporarily.

Men, on the other hand, have no such dichotomous pushing and pulling within. They may have a strong sex drive, but once they have satisfied that drive, they are free to go, leaving women with the important work. And go they often do.

Women's problems with their own commitment anxieties are

further compounded by the numbers game they must play in the world of love, relationships, and breeding. Simply put, the older a woman gets, the harder it is to find a tolerable mate (even an intolerable one), and the greater the risks of child-bearing. Therefore, even if her commitmentphobic impulses are screaming, "Put it off, put it off," the voice of reason is always countering with, "If you don't grab this one, you may never have another chance."

This, again, is not a problem for most men. If a man has the slightest desire to avoid or postpone commitment, he can always justify his actions. "I really have no deadlines," he thinks. "Even when I'm fifty I can always find a younger woman, settle down, and have a family." Essentially, his "numbers game" gives him the luxury of remaining "free," if he so desires.

Another significant factor that stops women from running is the fear of being alone. In a society that is still dominated by men it is difficult, and sometimes dangerous, to be a woman—especially a single woman. As a result, many women feel that they *need* to make a permanent commitment to a man, be it for safety, financial security, or simply to avoid loneliness. And typically, they are willing to make this commitment even if they really don't want to. Somehow, they figure, they will adjust. Unfortunately, most men who have this same problem do no such figuring.

Chapter 4

THE MAN AND HIS CONFLICT: A WORLD OF DOUBLE MESSAGES AND CONTRADICTORY BEHAVIOR

The commitmentphobic is a man of two minds, each with a distinct and separate point of view. One wants to be in a good relationship with a woman who loves him. The other views a permanent relationship as a suffocating trap. Chances are that in any given situation both of these totally contradictory points of view will somehow be expressed. To be involved with a commitmentphobic is to enter into a strange world of double messages and contradictory behavior. He can't give a clear yes, and he can't say no. If you are involved with such a man, you may recognize some of these characteristics. For example:

■ When it comes to your relationship, does he say one thing and do another?

■ Does he make and break plans?

■ Does he vacillate and change his mind?

■ Does he make promises he doesn't keep?

■ For every step forward, does he take two back?

PAYING ATTENTION: THE MOST IMPORTANT THING A WOMAN CAN DO TO PROTECT HERSELF EMOTIONALLY

I am extremely sympathetic to women who get involved with men with commitment problems. I know that more often than not the man overcomes a woman's resistance and natural caution by the enthusiasm of his pursuit. I also know that most of these men leave a trail of evidence concerning their commitmentphobic tendencies. Women are often guilty of not paying attention to this evidence.

The First Clue: His History with Other Women

Get rid of the idea that the man can be changed by the love of a good woman (and that you are that good woman).

Every woman has done it: She meets a man who reeks of commitmentphobia. His history with women is atrocious! But instead of listening to her good instincts, she listens to him. When he tells her about his problems in other relationships, she feels sorry for him. She assumes that the "other women" have been to blame. She tells herself that he will be different with her. Granted, at the beginning, he is often *telling* her that it will be different with her. However, a woman should not be so quick to assume that the man who is wooing her can be trusted to make good on his alleged intentions. If he has a questionable history with other women, she should pay attention, and protect herself accordingly.

MYTH: The man can be changed by the love of a good woman.
FACT: Most of the women he has met have been good women, and he has been unkind to all of them.

Other Clues: How He Is with You

Sometimes you can't judge from a man's history. Instead, the first inkling of trouble you get is when he starts creating it in your life, telling you one thing and doing another, not showing up for dates, or behaving differently and less attentively than he did at the beginning.

Typically a woman tends to not pay sufficient attention to these early warning signs of trouble in the relationship. She listens to the message she wants to hear and rationalizes away the one that is unpleasant. Her friends may warn her, but instead of listening, she becomes more protective of the man.

A woman has dozens of ways of avoiding what is happening

in a relationship with a commitmentphobic until it is too late to either protect herself or try to alter the outcome. By the time the man starts treating her badly, she may be totally confused about what is going on. Without insight, she may feel paralyzed, unable to do anything but hope that a miracle will occur and he will change. I hope this chapter, which talks about some of the more common ways a man may fool himself and/or the women he meets, will help provide some of this insight.

Although the underlying motivation is the same, every commitmentphobic is unique. Depending on his anxiety threshold, his family history, his economic background, and a dozen other psychosocial factors, the way in which each of these men gets his conflicting messages across may be slightly different. Here are some of the more common ways a man acts out his commitmentphobic conflict.

HE CAN'T COMMIT TO YES/HE CAN'T COMMIT TO NO

The most important thing to understand about the man who suffers from commitmentphobia is that *commitment* is the problem. What this means is that when it comes to relationships, he has as much trouble committing himself to no as he does committing himself to yes. Typically, when he is involved with a woman he cannot make the leap and agree to give the relationship his best shot, but he also cannot commit himself to walking away. Whichever choice he tries to make, he feels trapped and boxed in and anxious by his decision.

Consequently, he chooses not to choose. Or he vacillates. Or he goes one way and then he goes another. It's mind-boggling and maddening. These contradictions are part and parcel of a commitmentphobic's behavior pattern.

Cheryl, a twenty-eight-year-old travel agent, is genuinely confused by her boyfriend's contradictory behavior:

"I don't understand Alan. We're supposed to be having a relationship, but he never sees me. He calls every day and asks me out at least twice a week. Then, he doesn't show up for any of these dates—which *he* makes. He calls about an hour before he is supposed to arrive, always with an extraordinarily elaborate excuse. He tells me how much he wants to see me, hangs up, and then repeats the whole process the following week. It's truly amazing. Every now and then he manages to make it to my house. When he arrives, usually late, something is always wrong, he can't really stay—his back hurts, his mother needs him, his daughter needs him, his car needs repairing. When I ask him why he does this, he either gets angry or he promises not to do it anymore—a promise he doesn't keep. I won't agree to meet him anyplace anymore because there have been too many times when he hasn't showed up. When he started to act this way, I used to get upset because I missed him, and wanted to see him. But I don't even care anymore. I don't understand it, though. If he wants to see me, why doesn't he see me? If he doesn't, why doesn't he just say so and forget the whole thing?"

A man such as Alan is a good example of commitmentphobic vacillation. He is caught between conflicting impulses. When he is without Cheryl, he wants to be with her—he may even feel he loves her. But the moment he comes near, he feels trapped. That trapped feeling sends his fight or flight phobic response system into action, so he runs away and doesn't show up as planned. Then, relieved of the sense of entrapment, he is once more free to miss Cheryl, and the whole process is repeated.

SEDUCTIVE/REJECTIVE BEHAVIOR—THE COMMITMENTPHOBIC TRADEMARK

He is the most tender lover in the world; he is your best friend; nobody cares more about you or understands you better. That is, until he rejects you. The commitmentphobic's specialty is seduction and rejection. It is part and parcel of the pursuit/panic syndrome. Knowing this is small consolation for the woman who is the recipient of the rejection part.

Jan is a twenty-eight-year-old actress who entered therapy when her relationship with Martin, a doctor, ended.

"When Martin and I met, he practically followed me around. I thought he was going to lose his practice! He just couldn't see enough of me. Then, after about four months, he seemed less available. At first I liked it—I thought it meant the relationship was becoming more settled, more normal. Then suddenly he was less sexual. I assumed he was tired or thinking of work. After the way he had been with me, only a week or two before, it didn't occur to me that he had lost interest in me. He started to make excuses about having to sleep alone because he had surgery the next morning. After a couple of weeks, I was beginning to feel really rejected. I knew it couldn't be just fatigue. After a month, I felt as though he was trying to start an argument. You have to understand that the reason I was slow to react was that at the beginning, if anything, he was overly attentive physically. It was hard for me to believe that anyone could have changed that much. I kept trying to find excuses for his behavior. Also, I didn't want to appear demanding. Finally I saw we should talk. Well, when we talked, he agreed with me. He said he knew it wasn't fair. It was really interesting: he managed to turn the whole relationship around. He had turned into a reluctant lover and acted as if the beginning had never happened. I cried, and he finally said that he thought we shouldn't see each other anymore because I was becoming too upset. Believe me, I *was* upset. I called him and called him. I just couldn't believe what he was doing. He told me that he didn't want to talk to me anymore until I could control my feelings. He sounded so cold and cruel when he said that.

"The way in which he pursued me and then turned off was so unfair. Fortunately, in my business I get a lot of positive reinforcement about the way I look. Otherwise I don't think I would have been able to handle it. I kept thinking about all the things about my body that might have turned him off . . . It was really crazy."

Jan's initial reaction to Martin's rejection is fairly standard. The woman often responds with disbelief. She thinks it's impossible that he can really be this way with *her*. After all, this is the same man who was so intimate with her, so close, so together.

My best advice to such a woman: Believe it! Don't hang around to ask questions. Don't assume he is having a nervous break-down. Don't assume that there has been some sort of misunderstanding and that once he understands, everything will be all right again. And, of course, most importantly, don't think you did something wrong.

RATIONALIZATIONS—HIS WAY OF TELLING HIMSELF THAT MS. RIGHT IS MS. WRONG

None of us likes to admit that the way we handle our relationships is wrong. The commitmentphobic is no different. When he is hurtful, which he often is, he doesn't want to admit it. If he is foolish, he doesn't want to see it. If he is frightened, which he certainly is, he doesn't want to deal with it.

The commitmentphobic consistently deals with women in the same way and makes the same mistakes time and time again. Even so, like most of us, he wants to find some reasonable explanation for what goes wrong. Because he doesn't want to feel that *he* always destroys his chances for love, he needs an explanation to make him feel better about what he does. He needs a justification or rationalization to explain why he always needs to get out of a relationship.

Since no woman is perfect, the commitmentphobic doesn't have to look far to find a rationalization that will make him feel better about getting out of any relationship. He genuinely wants to believe that the commitment anxiety he is feeling is limited to this specific woman. This particular knee-jerk reaction is the classic, "It can't be me, so it must be her." All he has to do is take a look at the woman he's been involved with and find something wrong with her; then he can tell himself that he has a good reason for not wanting to commit. If you look hard enough, you can find a flaw in any woman; the commitmentphobic uses these flaws to help him rationalize his need to escape. It can be the smallest of imperfections—the way a fork is held, the way a word is mispronounced, a ripple on a thigh, a small wrinkle under the eye—anything that will confuse the issue and help him get out and forgive himself for his behavior.

Throughout this book you will see examples of men who rationalize their inability to commit by finding fault with the woman.

These men can never find the perfect woman; something is always wrong. What is most amazing is that the "something" that is wrong is almost always a quality that was present and obvious when the man began his pursuit.

A good example is the man who pursues a dancer and then rejects her because she has no head for business. When you look at it from afar, it's mildly humorous. But if you are the woman who is being dissected and examined for failings, it doesn't feel funny.

Gregory, a free-lance photographer, is honest enough to admit that he does this:

"Look, I think it happens when a part of me wants to get out of the relationship, and I don't have the guts to just be straight about it . . . so I pick apart the woman. Whenever I meet someone I like, at the beginning, she can do no wrong. I think every little quirk is adorable. I know that I do this. I also know that later on, the same things I found cute I start to despise. I know I start this because I'm trying to make sure the relationship doesn't work—I've done it too many times, with too many nice women."

A BUILT-IN EXCUSE FOR FAILURE—HE ALWAYS CHOOSES MS. WRONG

And then there is the commitmentphobic who manages to disguise *his* problem by always choosing women who *are* totally wrong or inappropriate for him.

Sometimes these women are clearly inappropriate choices. For example, there is too great an age difference or there is an obvious religious conflict. Other times, they just have views and attitudes that are diametrically opposed to everything the commitmentphobic would tell you that he wants in a woman. Either way, these inappropriate choices provide the man who wants to get out with ample reasons and excuses for doing so.

Adam, a high-powered stockbroker, is a good example. By any standard, Adam is a "catch." Everybody is always fixing him up with charming, lovely, intelligent women who are prepared to adore him. Adam is never interested; he claims these women are boring. The women he has not found boring include an eighteen-year-old young Spanish woman with a very traditional family who will not allow her to go out with Adam, and a very wealthy and pampered married woman who even he admits is selfish and not too bright. However, he said, he would have married her in an instant.

One time Adam did get involved with someone who could have been right for him. She was a young lawyer—the same age, the same interests, the same friends. Adam says that he "thought" he loved her at the time, but he felt he couldn't marry her because she was a spendthrift. This is, by the way, a quality that he admits he shares, but he feels that he would want a wife who would balance him in this area.

ONE DATE, NO MORE

He's lonely, yet he refuses to do anything about it because he thinks every woman wants to marry him. Nowhere is the commitmentphobic's conflict more obvious than it is with the man who screams of loneliness, yet is unable to make the slightest move toward a relationship. Often this man is so terrified that, as far as he is concerned, a dinner date with an attractive woman is tantamount to announcing his engagement. To his confused head, a second date implies that marriage is expected of him. No matter how long he's known the woman or how casually they have met, if he's strongly attracted to her, he immediately starts thinking of marriage. Frightened by even the thought, he ends it, right there. A man such as this may know that he can't make a permanent commitment, and be really sincere about not wanting to use or mislead a woman by allowing a relationship to develop further. Arthur is a good example of such a man.

A good-looking and genuinely likeable thirty-four-year-old plastic surgeon, Arthur has many friends, both male and female, but he hasn't had a relationship with a woman for close to five years. He is acutely aware of his problems with commitment:

"I've been reluctant about getting involved with every woman I've ever met except one, and she was living with another guy and wasn't really interested in me . . . so she hardly counts. When I meet a new woman I'm attracted to, I'm like the advertising executive who comes in with one thing to sell—me. But once I know I've made the sale, which usually happens the first evening, I'm off. I look at a woman I've just met, and instead of thinking about taking her to a movie, I'm worried about how I'll feel about her in ten years. I actually think things like, 'It may be fine now, but I'll get bored, and I won't want to be with her anymore, and then there'll have to be a divorce, and what about the kids? I know it's crazy, but that's how I think. A friend of mine says I spend my life avoiding women who would be right for me.

"I find that within the first hour I start talking about the possibility of moving to another city. I always want an excuse to get away if I want to, so I tell women I'm on call and may have to leave, as though somebody could want me, and the conversation could be interrupted, and I could be gone in a second.

"You know, this doesn't work to my benefit either. I'm thirty-four years old. I haven't been out with a woman more than once for the last two years. I don't sleep with women on the first date. You figure it out. I'm not happy this way, but the alternative seems to provoke so much anxiety. Ideally, my relationships should be like seasonal homes—you know, a winter relationship,' a summer relationship, each one providing what the other doesn't. Yet I know I couldn't seriously go out with more than one woman at a time.

"When I think of getting married, I worry that my life will be over. I don't want to lose my lifestyle, which in my case often turns out to be going home, watching television alone, and reheating an old slice of pizza. It's not terrific, but I feel as if the alternative would be like being stuck for all eternity within an airless room.

"Recently I met a woman I really liked. We had a wonderful evening, but I never followed through with anything romantic. Then, five months later, I was on a trip, and I saw something that reminded me of her. So I sent it to her, with a card. She is probably walking around right now thinking, 'This guy is weird, he does all these nice things, but he never asks me out. I wonder why.' "

DISTANCING: A COMMITMENTPHOBIC TOOL

Since a commitmentphobic wants both a relationship and space, what better way to try to have it all than to always get involved with women who live far, far away? For this man, distance relieves anxiety, at least temporarily. A woman who gets involved with a man such as this often ends up feeling totally devastated. It's hard for her to understand why a man who adored her in Antigua doesn't want to see her on his home turf. From his vantage point, the closer she gets, the worse he feels.

The long-distance lover

The commitmentphobic who works his relationships long-distance is one of the most romantic and seductive of men. Actual physical space separates him from the woman; hence, he doesn't need to create emotional distance. Because, in his head, the relationship is by definition limited, he is able to indulge in his feelings of love and tenderness. The rules governing long-distance love imply that he can only see the woman at certain times. Consequently he feels much less threatened, and thinks that he always has a built-in excuse to end it. This is, of course, not necessarily true, but it's the way he feels.

If you are a woman involved with a long-distance commitmentphobic, you may discover that the romance can disappear overnight if you literally move closer or try to change the rules and see him more often.

Tom, who we met in the last chapter, says that he knows that he overindulges romantically when the woman lives far away:

"I seem to always prefer being separated from the women I love. I swear it started back in camp when I would wait until the last three or four days before I would decide which girl I liked. Then I would quickly move in, push away the competition, and by the last day we would be 'going steady.' I'd go home, pine over her, write letters and phone when my parents let me. This would last for a couple of months. After a few months, I would have forgotten about her. But she would still be writing letters I wouldn't answer, and I would wonder why. It's not so different now.

"I remember one woman who lived in Los Angeles. I met

her at a conference, and we seemed to really get along. When I got back home to New York, I wrote her a letter and invited her to come with me on a vacation to the Caribbean. She accepted. We had a great time, sitting on the beach until two or three in the morning, talking, making love. It was really great. When I got back, I phoned often and asked her to come to New York. She did. She ended up coming to New York like once every two months for over a year. I was seeing other women at the time, but none of them was as important to me as she was. I knew she was beginning to wonder where the relationship was going. I think that made me realize that I didn't want to be with her for the rest of my life. It was just a lot of little things. Although I had been very attracted to her at the beginning, she had never really been my physical type. Just as she began to push for more, I knew I was losing interest. In the meantime, I never had been to visit her in L.A. It was Thanksgiving, and I decided I was going to go to San Francisco to visit my college roommate. Well, she got furious. She said that she had gone out of her way dozens of times to come to New York, and not only was I not spending Thanksgiving with her, but this was proof that I never went out of my way to come and see her—even though I could go out of my way to visit a friend. We had a terrible fight on the phone. I didn't call her back. A couple of months later I got a card from her, and we talked a few times, but that was that."

A special variation on the long-distance lover is the commit-mentphobic I refer to as "Club Med Fred." His specialty is vacation romance, with *absolutely no follow-through*. Unless he is on a trip, and away from his own environment, he never gets involved. But put this man on the road, and watch out: he is hot stuff when he thinks he has a built-in reason why he may never see the woman again. Don't let his name fool you—he isn't always found on a beach wearing a Hawaiian print shirt. You can find him in tweed at an academic conference, or in grey flannel at a business meeting. His only criterion is that you and he are ships that pass in the night. And in his mind, the key word is "pass."

HOUDINI—THE DISAPPEARING ACT

What could be more confusing than the man who tells a woman he wants a commitment—and then disappears?

The legendary Harry Houdini was known as the Great Escape Artist, the man who couldn't be tied or bound. The modern-day Houdini practically invites the woman to tie him up. Then, avoiding commitment at any cost, he breaks free from tender emotional bonds as skillfully as Harry Houdini did from ensnaring ropes and chains.

If you are unfortunate enough to meet a Houdini, this is the man who pursues you, romances you, never gives in until he wins your heart. Then he vanishes. But in the beginning, nothing about him appears reluctant. He practically begs you to tie him up. You, the naive volunteer from the audience, willingly go along with his request. Then, just as his name implies, he slips the bonds and disappears from your life. He may reappear again, but when he does, the situation is completely changed.

This is a man who likes to take curtain calls, so it's best to leave the theater after his initial performance; if you've seen the trick once, it's enough. Staying around is not going to give you any insight into how or why it's done.

Marie, a thirty-six-year-old speech pathologist from Long Island, met a classic Houdini about two years ago. Here's her story. Learn from it!

"I'm embarrassed that I was so stupid and so naive, but here's what happened. I met Glen on a highway. I was driving back from upstate where my daughter goes to school. He passed me in a Lincoln Continental and sort of looked me over. Then he must have slowed down because I passed him. About twenty miles later I stopped. He pulled in right behind me at Howard Johnson's. I was getting coffee to take out, and he got in line behind me. He smiled. I smiled. He was attractive, he looked nice, and he was well dressed. This may all be superficial but when you meet somebody on a highway, what else can you go by?

"Anyway, he came over to me and we talked in the parking lot for a long time. He managed to share quite a lot about himself and was much more open than I was. He said he was divorced and was some kind of heavy manager with a company in New Jersey, right near the bridge. He said it was a new job, and he was living with a friend in New York while he looked for an apartment. His ex-wife lived in their old house upstate. He gave me his card and asked me to call him, which I didn't do. About a week later, he called me at work. I had told him my first name and where I worked, and he had managed to track me down—which wasn't easy, believe me, because it's a big hospital.

"Well, he swept me off my feet. For the next two weeks he drove out to my house on Long Island every night, and then drove back to New York because I didn't want to rush into bed. He said he had fallen madly in love—he wanted to take care of me, take care of my daughter, do everything for me. After two weeks, I went to bed with him, and he proposed. I have to mention here that I've had a very tough time financially. My daughter is in a special school and I've had a lot of bills. Glen told me, and I saw no reason not to believe him, that he was very comfortable. I must admit that the prospect of someone shouldering some of my responsibilities was very inviting. He acted as though he wanted to marry me, and I believed him. Anyway, this whirlwind romance continued for another couple of weeks. I told everyone we were getting married, and he moved in with me.

"As soon as he moved in, his attitude changed. Suddenly he couldn't bear the forty-five-minute drive each way. A week before he was commuting both ways every night, and not complaining. But once he moved in, he was miserable about it—it was all he could talk about, every night. Then he started picking on me in a way that was so opposite to how he was before. For example, once in the car I drove the wrong way, and we were lost for about five minutes, and he became incredibly angry and started belittling me, telling me how stupid I was. Another time, I was standing in front of the closet trying to decide what to wear, and he looked at me and said, with real disgust, 'If you weren't overweight, it wouldn't be such a problem.'

"Then he said he got really angry with me because I had gone to bed with him so soon, and we argued about that for a while. This phase lasted only a few weeks, because suddenly it was Christmas, and we were supposed to go to his parents', upstate, for the holiday. I had never met them; as a matter of fact, I had never met any of his friends. I called him at work once so I know he worked where he said he worked, but I can't confirm anything else about it.

"Anyway, about two or three days before Christmas, I came home from work, and all of his stuff was cleared out, and there was a note on the refrigerator. It said: 'Something's come up. I'll call and explain it to you. I just can't handle things right now.' That was it. He was gone. I thought, 'He'll call me right away.' But he didn't call and didn't call. And I became frantic. I worried that something had happened to him. He drove fast. I worried that he was so upset that he was distracted and had an accident. I realized that if something happened to him, nobody would know to call me. I thought something awful must have happened—otherwise I was sure he would have called me.

"I went through every scrap of paper in the house trying to find some way of reaching him. Finally, on an old phone bill, I spotted a number that he must have phoned in upstate New York. I called it and reached a friend of his. I just explained that I was distraught. The friend obviously was able to reach Glen because later that night Glen phoned. He was furious at me for 'tracking him down.' He said that his ex-wife was trying to tie up some property, and he just couldn't handle everything at once. He said, 'I just can't do this.'

"He was the one who had pushed the whole relationship; he made me tell my parents and friends about the marriage. He made me call the couple of men I had been dating and tell them I was getting married and couldn't see them anymore. I can't believe I did all this, but I guess I was flattered that somebody wanted to assume responsibility for me.

"In any event, I wrote him a long letter. I think it was pretty forgiving in tone—I just wanted an explanation for what had happened. Any explanation would have done, but I really wanted to know the truth. I said I thought I deserved some sort of explanation.

"About a month later, he phoned late one night. He basically apologized and said he couldn't handle the relationship—it had been going too fast. He said that he wanted me to forgive him, and that he wanted to see me again. I said no because I had very bad feelings about what had happened. I had been very unhappy.

"I know I should have been more skeptical in the beginning, but women like to believe in miracles. I wanted to go along with what he was telling me and believe that this was like a movie romance."

Not all Houdini episodes are as dramatic as the one Marie experienced with Glen, but they are never subtle. Houdini is the worst-case example of a commitmentphobic who gets in over his head and suddenly panics. All he wants is to get away. He doesn't want to have discussions, and he doesn't want to try to work the problem out. He realizes that it is very hard to justify his behavior, but he doesn't care.

He disappears because he knows if he stops long enough to tell the woman what he is feeling, she will suggest that they try to work the problem out. This is exactly what he doesn't want to do. He just wants to get away, and his discomfort is so great that he cannot and will not allow anything to slow down his escape process.

The men I've spoken to describe this experience as being akin to being drunk and sobering up. They are heady with the experience of new love and plunge forward without thinking. Then, one day, also with no thought, they claim they sober up and know they have to renege on their commitment.

After the fact, these men typically feel guilty and embarrassed and want to forget the whole experience. The women are often wiped out—and always want some form of explanation.

The "Now-You-See-Him, Now-You-Don't" Houdini

This is a variation on the typical Houdini theme. In these instances, Houdini disappears and reappears regularly over an extended period of time—sometimes years. Here's an example:

Monica met Jerry at a party in the spring. By the end of June, they were talking about combining households as well as careers.

They were both travel agents, and he encouraged her to think that they would go into business together. She actually went so far as to start looking for office space. Then, after spending the Fourth of July weekend together with Monica's eight-year-old daughter at her family's house in the Berkshires, Jerry drove home and didn't call again. Monica made several attempts to get in touch with him, but—not wanting to seem pathetic—she stopped after a few unanswered phone calls. Jerry showed up again on Thanksgiving. His excuse: He left in July because his feelings for her were so intense he didn't know how to handle them. Although he said he didn't want to run anymore, he ran again on Christmas Eve, ruining Monica's holiday and forcing her to spend Christmas Day hiding her tears from her child. Jerry showed up again in May. . . . This has now been going on for two years. Monica knows she shouldn't allow it, but their time together is so perfect that she keeps believing and hoping that Jerry has changed and that there will be no repeat performances.

Leaving When the Going Gets Good—One Step Forward Equals Two Steps Back

We can all understand men who leave bad relationships. Commitmentphobics, however, have a tendency to leave, or run, when the going gets good. If one of these men spends a close, intimate, and joy-filled weekend with a woman who loves him, he often comes away from it in a state of panic. As far as he is concerned, such a weekend implies that something more will eventually be expected of him. After all, he reasons to himself, how many perfect weekends can a relationship sustain without the woman wanting more?

This sort of logic often encourages him to put distance into the relationship. He may be having the best time ever, but instead of wanting to see the woman more, he may decide that he wants to see her less because he doesn't want the relationship to get into the commitment groove.

The woman with whom he's been having such a terrific time rarely understands his convoluted logic. Greta's reaction is a common one:

"I knew my relationship with Daniel was in trouble after

we took our first long weekend together. We had a marvelous time, and I came back head over heels in love. He seemed to feel the same way. When we reached my apartment, I expected him to want to come in—we hadn't been separated for almost five days. I thought he would want that feeling to continue, like I did. He said he was tired. Then he didn't call for two days. I phoned him once, because I really missed him, and he sounded cool. He didn't ask me out again until the following Sunday night. It was too long since I'd seen him. It was a clear message to me that he hadn't enjoyed our closeness as much as I had, and it told me in no uncertain terms that this man didn't want the relationship to grow."

Greta is a very strong, and experienced, woman. She was able to evaluate Daniel's behavior and distance herself before she got hurt. Many women are not so immediately perceptive. They sense that something is wrong, but they try to accept the commitmentphobic's boundaries and time limitations, thinking that time will conquer his fear. This is almost always a mistake.

The man who is able to make a commitment rarely does this kind of dancing back and forth. He may move slowly, but he continues to move in the same direction.

CHANGING HIS MIND

Why would a man go so far as to propose if he wasn't sincere? I've heard so many stories about a commitmentphobic proposing and then changing his mind that it seems to have sort of an epidemic quality. In some cases, he did it within days. In others, he waited until after wedding invitations were sent. No matter how far along the wedding plans have progressed, it stands to reason that the woman is devastated.

But when plans have gone forward, not only does she have to deal with the pain involved, she also often has other considerations. One woman told me that her parents had already spent several thousand dollars on wedding invitations and a nonrefundable down payment on a hall, etc. Even if no money has been spent, the woman still has to face the world and tell her friends and family what happened. Often she can't explain what happened, and she knows that no matter what she says, some people are going to assume that *she* did something to make *him* change his mind.

Don, a doctor who proposed and backed out, isn't sure himself what happened. Like many commitmentphobics, he knows that he was lured by the notion of making a commitment. He says he was discouraged by his dating habits, and he genuinely wanted to be able to be mature enough to settle into a permanent relationship, but it didn't work out that way. Here's his story:

"When I met Sara, I hadn't had an ongoing relationship for years. I was literally going out with hundreds of different women, and everyone was pointing out how outrageous I was. I was tired of the perpetual dating, as well as of hearing about it. I met Sara at a health club on Tuesday. I was wildly attracted to her and called the next day and asked if she wanted a spur-of-the-moment movie date. I remember that I asked her if we could "pretend to be like a normal couple and go to a movie and eat popcorn"! I guess I must have liked her because I started seeing her almost every night.

"After about six weeks of this, in the middle of the night in a totally romantic mood, without thinking of the ramifications of what I was saying, I proposed, and she said yes. The next morning when I woke up, I felt awful. I had this horrible feeling in my stomach, like oh, no, you've made a *terrible, terrible* mistake. I felt the same way you feel when you're scared . . . a panicked feeling in my stomach. I thought I was going to be sick. In the meantime, she was flying around the apartment, singing like a bird, and I was unable to move. I went to work very moody and quiet. I don't remember doing this, but my friends tell me I called them and told them that I had gotten engaged. Maybe I wanted to prove to them that I *could* get engaged. My proposal was totally inappropriate. I hadn't known her long enough.

"When I proposed I didn't find anything wrong with Sara, and I might have gone through with it except that her behavior also became suspect. For example, I don't think a normal girl would have said yes to someone she only knew six weeks. The only excuse was that she was mad for me, which she was, and I tried to remember that. I don't know . . . all I know is that

I didn't want to get married, and the more she sensed my hesitations, the more she pressed to go forward with the planning. She told her parents and her sisters, and I thought, 'How dare she tell them, how dare she give them control over my life.' The next weekend, for the first time since I met her, I wanted to be alone to do my thing . . . I wanted to go out with friends and play tennis and relax.

"We started fighting, and we broke the engagement and ended the relationship within months. Sometimes I see her in my neighborhood, and I'm tempted to try and start up again . . . but I know better.

"I was very attracted to Sara and we had a terrific time together; I felt no panic until I proposed. But it's always easy for me until I commit; then I start looking for faults because I'm thinking, can I live with this person for the rest of my life? When you start thinking about it that way, you start worrying about being trapped. I think, will I spend the rest of my life being exasperated by this person?

"If I could give women one word of advice, I would tell them to watch out for the man who goes head over heels quickly, because as quickly as he pursues, that's just how fast he retreats."

WHEN HE WANTS TO LEAVE, BUT HE CAN'T SAY SO

When these men want to leave a relationship, they are rarely able to come out and say so. Instead, they continue to say, "I love you," but they begin to exhibit their conflict by behaving peculiarly when they are with you. In these instances, body language can tell a lot.

Body Language 101

Sleep Patterns

Both the men and the women I have interviewed have commented upon odd sleeping behavior that they felt was reflective of the commitment conflict. Maureen, an editorial assistant, remembers the way her ex-boyfriend, Bob, conveyed his conflict through the way he slept.

"Bob and I had an on-again/off-again relationship for years. I could always tell when he was about to go off again by the way he slept with me—not the sex, but the sleeping itself. In the beginning, he would always sleep comfortably curled around me. We would wake up and have breakfast together. But when he was withdrawing, he would complain he couldn't fall asleep. When he did finally fall asleep, it would be on the far side of the bed. He would also start waking earlier and earlier. I remember one of the final cycles. It was three-thirty in the morning, it was pitch black outside, and there was Bob coming out of the shower and getting dressed for work. I thought he was sleepwalking. It was obvious that he couldn't get out of there fast enough."

Here are some of the sleep patterns that may reflect commitment anxiety. Many of these seem pretty humorous in the telling, but all of these have been attested to by many of the women, and men, I interviewed.

1. Does he get up and sleep in another bed or on the couch?
2. Does he have trouble sleeping in your bed?
3. Does he ever push you out of bed in his sleep?
4. Does he alternate between hugging you and shoving you all night long?
5. Does he leave in the middle of the night?
6. Does he never let you sleep at his place?
7. Does he almost never sleep at your place?
8. Does he never have time for breakfast?
9. Is your bed the only place in the world where he can't sleep?
10. Is his bed too small for two people ever to sleep on comfortably?

Hand in Hand, But Not Necessarily Together
"I should have known he'd never walk with me down the aisle . . . he couldn't even walk with me down the street."

Similar sentiments have been expressed by an amazing number of women I talked to. Walking is a simple act. Millions of people do it every day. But it would appear that even something as simple as a stroll down the block seems painful for the commitmentphobic when it's with the woman he can't love. He can convey his need for distance in dozens of simple ways—the way he sits near you, stands with you, enters a room beside you. If he feels trapped and wants to get away, it shows. Ask yourself these questions:

1. Does he always walk too fast for you to catch up?

2. Does he change his pace whenever you think you have finally adapted your pace to his?

3. Does he zigzag away from you while walking?

4. Does he seem uncomfortable when he must sit close to you—at the movies, theaters, etc.?

5. Does he abandon you at parties and go to the other side of the room?

6. Is he comfortable when engaging in sports activities with you such as tennis, bicycling, dancing, skiing?

7. Is he comfortable sharing indoor activities with you? For example, can you cook together, clean together, do laundry together?

8. Is he comfortable going to a supermarket and food-shopping with you?

SEXUAL COMMITMENTPHOBIA—HOT PANTS, COLD FEET

Men know that even in the post–Sexual Revolution world, women do not take sex that lightly. Men know that a sexual relationship with a single woman of an appropriate age cannot go on forever without something else being expected. That something else is commitment. Therefore, to many a commitmentphobic, no matter how much he may want it, an ongoing sexual relationship is going to provoke the willies.

In his distorted logic, the goal is to make sure the woman never expects commitment. There are several familiar ploys which are used to sustain a sense of insecurity and keep the woman off balance. He just doesn't want the woman to expect anything more than what he is capable of giving at the moment. As odd as it may seem, many times he is only trying not to lead the woman on.

Tonight You're Mine Completely

One of the most thoughtless games a commitmentphobic plays revolves around one perfect night of love. In this game, the commitmentphobic spends the night wooing and winning the woman. On this night he carries on as if he is open, he is tender, he is sensitive, he is caring, he has noble values, he has honest emotions. He probably leads the woman to believe that this night is the first of many. And he believes it, too, at the time. Then he never calls her again, leading the woman to think God knows what!

When a woman is treated this way she feels demoralized and dehumanized. It can make her wonder whether she did something or whether there was something about her that could have turned him off. I've heard women wonder if he has been in an auto accident. Why else would he not call? In some cases, the one night of love followed weeks of wooing in person and on the phone. The woman honestly believed she was starting a real relationship. Incidentally, as you can see in the following man's story, it doesn't even matter whether or not the sexual act is completed.

"I could fall in love at least once a month, and sometimes do. The other night was a good example. I was with the woman, a blind date. We went to dinner, and then I took her dancing. It was romantic. I really got into her—she was very good-looking, and sweet as sugar. We went back to her place and we necked on her living room floor for hours. It was spectacular, and very romantic. She didn't want me to spend the night because she has a small daughter, and she said we didn't know each other that well. As I was leaving, I asked her if I could call her again. She said, 'You'd better.'

"I decided not to take her out again. There are too many things wrong. I don't want to marry her, and she wants marriage, I can tell. I do this all the time. I just find too many things wrong with everyone. You have to know your own heart, and I never know my own heart. I look at every woman and think not only of the things I might find wrong with her one day, but also of all the things my family and my friends might find wrong with her. Sometimes I don't think I'll ever get married—I said this to a friend of mine last week, and he said he didn't believe it. He said he thought I was just very picky, and he made it sound like it was an asset, so I bought him dinner and a zillion drinks because it was what I wanted to hear. But I have to tell you the truth: I could be with seven different women on seven different nights and think each of them was great when I was with her, and then go on to the next and tell her she's great, and then never take any of them out again because I started to find fault with them. I always call everyone, even if I don't take them out. I tell them I'm busy and have a lot to do . . . then I call again in a few weeks. Eventually they get the message."

Let's Be Friends

This is a variation on "Tonight You're Mine Completely." In this case, the commitmentphobic does the traditional wooing and winning. After the night of love, however, the man does phone within a few days or a week to ask the woman out again. When he sees her, he makes a point of not sleeping with her. He usually has some perfectly plausible reason for having to be home early.

The woman ultimately still feels rejected. But she also feels confused. There has been a change somewhere that she doesn't understand. He starts out wanting to be her lover, but ends up developing just a friendship with a sexual undertone—which he never, or rarely and perfunctorily, follows through on. The logic in this is much the same as in "Tonight You're Mine . . . ," with one major difference. When "Let's Be Friends" follows "Tonight You're Mine," the man often has a hidden agenda—another woman with whom he is involved. In the meantime the woman with whom he wants to be friends keeps wondering why he stopped wanting to sleep with her.

More Frightened Than Fulfilled

Remember that the commitmentphobic is extremely ardent at the beginning—and he may stay that way. But if he is a true commitmentphobic, and you reach the middle stage of the relationship, there will probably be a shift in his behavior. This can be very subtle—he doesn't have to lose interest in sex, or in you. But his attitude is different. Where once he was romantic, now he's clinical. Where once he was a shy fumbling schoolboy, now he's a sexual master. There is a definite and noticeable change, and it's not just because everything has gotten more relaxed.

He may also have very subtly turned you into the more aggressive partner. This shift is so amazing that it's almost as though it is done with mirrors. He starts out so overwhelmed by you that he is insecure in your presence, and he may end up acting as though you talked him into it.

Paul, a forty-year-old teacher, talks about the sexual change that occurred in his two-year affair with Linda:

"When I knew in my heart I wasn't going to marry Linda, everything changed for me sexually. It wasn't that I was any less attracted to her, but I felt guilty. The guilt made it impossible for me to be as free as I had been just a few weeks before. I knew that if I was going to get out of the relationship without hurting her badly, one of the first areas in which I had to pull back was sexually. It's not that I stopped sleeping with her, but I stopped spending as much time in bed, and I was willing to let evenings go by. It was easier for me to justify having sex with her if she initiated it. That way I didn't feel as if I was leading her on as much. Sometimes it was very strange. We would be in incredibly romantic circumstances, and that made me withdraw even more because I was worried that we would have a terrific evening, and we'd be right back where we started, and she would have a reason for thinking we were going to get married."

MEANINGLESS TEARS

I don't know if commitmentphobics cry more than anybody else, but so many women have mentioned episodes of crying that I started questioning men about it. Sure enough, from the people I've spoken to, it would appear that these men are most likely to cry under the following conditions:

■ *At the very beginning—on the first or second date.*
An amazing number of women have told me that these men are apt to have tears come to their eyes early in the relationship. This usually happens when he is telling the woman some "sensitive" tale about his life or displaying his emotions on some subject. I don't mean to be cynical about this, but I must admit that I find it extraordinary that these men are so able to open up this way with strangers. The message that is conveyed to the woman is: I trust you with my feelings, and I want you to trust me. She usually does.

■ *In the middle, when he promises to change, and doesn't.*
The second time these men cry is in the Middle. If the woman is fed up with the commitmentphobic's ups and downs, she may try to end the relationship. When this happens, he may throw himself on her mercy, promising to change. Often at this point, he cries.

This is not so difficult to understand. Remember, if he got to the middle of a relationship, he is genuinely involved with the woman. Since he is also genuinely in conflict, his commitment anxieties are probably playing havoc with his emotions and are making him hypersensitive to everything. His panic is making him lose control of his emotions; he doesn't want to lose the woman as well, even though she is exacerbating his anxiety.

Paul, who described his sexual withdrawal from Linda, remembers when he cried:

"Linda was fed up. We'd been together about two years and I was no closer to marrying her than I had been at day one. I had also come on to a friend of hers, and she was pretty upset. She refused to answer my phone calls. She wouldn't even talk to me. I went over to her house and stood at her door while I pleaded with her to open up. When she did, I was crying. But even as I did it, I knew that I didn't know why. It was almost as if I thought maybe I would get hit on the head, and my whole perspective would change . . . like I would wake up one morning all grown up, and my needs and attitudes would be all different. I didn't want to take the chance of losing her should that happen, but at the same time I knew that if this major life shakeup didn't occur, there was no way I could stay with her for any period of time. It was pure selfishness. I wanted to know that she was there . . . just in case."

THE MAN WITH THE HIDDEN AGENDA—AN UNFAIR ADVANTAGE

Some commitmentphobics use a hidden agenda, which almost always involves another woman, to maintain distance. Exactly as the phrase implies, the hidden agenda is truly hidden. Consequently you have to look extra-hard to find it. A hidden agenda is always complicated; it is never fair.

I think the following example of a relationship with a hidden agenda is a good one, and one that women can learn from:

Teri's Story

Teri is an energetic, athletic blonde with a super personality and lots of charm. Her friends all love her because she's so good-natured and easy-going. There's no denying, however, that these qualities have contributed to some of the problems she has had with men. Teri was recently in a relationship that was doomed to fail. She knows it now because after the relationship ended, she was able to piece together the facts and find out what was really happening. But at the time, she didn't know what was going on. How could she? Jack, the man she was involved with, never gave her all the information she needed to take care of herself . . . or so it seemed at the time.

Everything about Teri's background is straight middle-class, middle America. Her family lives in Ohio, where her father was a respected judge; her mother was a French teacher. She was taught to tell the truth and to expect the truth. When Jack, a forty-five-year-old clinical psychologist, was introduced by friends, she saw no reason to "grill" him about everything he said, and she took what he said at face value. She assumed that everything

Jack said was totally honest. Why should she expect anything else?

If it's any consolation for Teri, she should know that Jack is no more or less honest with himself than he was with her. Jack is a commitmentphobic who always has a hidden agenda. What this means is that something else is always going on that keeps him from making a solid, honest attachment. Only Jack has all the facts at any one moment, and, to be perfectly fair, he doesn't intend to mislead anyone.

I interviewed Teri in the living room of the large Victorian house she shares with a roommate in a Boston suburb. Teri, who is a thirty-three-year-old nursery school teacher, had been kind enough to make me lunch—that's the kind of woman she is. I devoured it while she told me her story. As you read it, try to think of what she could have done to find out the truth from the beginning.

"Jack was introduced by a friend who had us both over to dinner. It was a very easy meeting, and although we got along, I wasn't that interested at first, but Jack was so interested in me that it was appealing. When you meet a new man and he seems to like you so much, you get more excited about it. I have to admit it—the fact that he liked me made me respect his judgment."

Teri laughed as she said this, and I asked her how he had indicated his interest.

"He really fooled me. Although he wasn't verbal, he was extraordinarily affectionate. Wherever we would walk, he would put his arm around me. He started calling me almost every day, and I knew where he was every night. He saw his children at least three nights a week, and he always told me what he was doing, and when he had his children; he seemed to want to see me whenever he was free. He had a lot of problems with his children and he told me all sorts of intimate details about his life. He said he had problems with his ex-wife who was still very jealous and kept tabs on him. Although he didn't say, 'I love you, I need you,' he sort of indicated through his actions that he wanted something more than just a casual relationship.

"It took us a while to get around to sex because I was dragging my heels, but he planned dates that were sort of logical progressions to sex. The second date we went dancing; he held my hand and as the night went on, we danced more closely together, and it became more sensual, more agreeable. He was so affectionate that the sex was just a slow, easy progression—it was very easy to get in to.

"I remember one Saturday afternoon date when I had to leave early. Jack was particularly amorous, and didn't want me to leave. But I wasn't particularly sure where I wanted the relationship to go. He didn't tell me he wanted something long-term, but he certainly implied it. I think it was two dates later when we slept together for the first time, and it was very nice.

"By this time, we were seeing each other three or four times a week, and he was calling me almost every day. He made a point of always telling me where he was going to be. He would ask me out on Tuesday, Thursday, and Saturday. Those were the nights he didn't have his kids.

"In any event, once we slept together, it changed. I sensed it immediately. We still saw each other as often, but he became different somehow—he had been very warm, very loving, and then he abruptly shut down. I wondered what I was doing. It made me very self-conscious, and I tried to discuss it, but he sort of brushed off my attempt. You know, when you're in a relationship that's still relatively new, you don't know the man that well. It could be anything; he had all these problems. I didn't want to be another problem, so I just tried to be supportive and understanding.

"But he got uncomfortable about sex. It was obvious. He didn't want me to sleep at his house and started leaving me at my door saying he had to see his children in the morning. It was apparent he didn't want to sleep with me anymore. He told me that it was because of his ex-wife, that he was very uncomfortable about sex. He said he still felt married. I felt sorry for him. He didn't want me to stay over in his apartment; he didn't want to stay over in mine. I was getting to like him very much—and I remember once calling him just to say hello, and I could tell it made him uncomfortable. He said his younger son told his wife that 'there's this woman Teri who keeps calling Dad.' This was obviously a big problem for him . . . I didn't pay much attention to it, but he made a big deal out of it. He indicated that it created a crisis with his children, and it made me uncomfortable about calling him.

"For whatever reason, the relationship was not turning out the way I would have hoped. I'm not aggressive, and I didn't argue with him or try to prolong it. I just said, let's forget it.

"At the beginning, I didn't realize how involved he was with his ex-wife. It wasn't clear to me at all. I knew he had a close relationship with the children, but he didn't mention his wife.

"When he talked about any of his wives, it was past tense . . . he was very guilty about them, particularly the first . . . very troubled. I think the second marriage was very short, and then he had a lot of problems with his third wife.

"But he was very warm, and he seemed very sensitive. I think he was a lovely person, and I still have good feelings about him. If I were to express my anger to him, I think I would want to say to him, 'Why did you start up with me? We didn't have to go to bed, we could have been friends . . . Why did you start up, then shut down, and say good-bye?' But it's hard to get really angry at him because I think he was screwed up. I don't think he intended things to end the way they did. I think he got scared.

"He wrote me a letter saying I deserved more and a better relationship than the one he could offer me. I called him, and he took me out to dinner, and I cried. I said that I was really sad that we couldn't have a relationship. He told me this story about how he rented an apartment, he rented a TV, he rented a car, that everything in his life was very temporary—he couldn't even make a commitment to buy anything. I felt very sorry for him because I don't think he wanted to hurt me. I don't think he dates much. He seems to be lonely, and he didn't like to be alone."

Teri didn't admit it to me, but I could tell that Jack's rejection pained her. Many women are not as fortunate as Teri. They don't have a supportive, loving family and a huge circle of friends.

They may have severe ego problems to start out with. But no matter how "together" a woman is, it is hurtful to have a man start a physical relationship and then back off. It makes her feel insecure and undesirable. She may wonder whether the man has some sexual problems. She may question whether she is being seductive enough. She may worry about his ego and whether she is making it clear that she wants him.

Jack is a good example of a man who was extremely seductive and sexual at the beginning, and then backed off. What went wrong?

In the case of Jack and Teri, I happened to know the couple who had introduced them, and they in turn contacted Jack, who agreed to tell me what had gone wrong from his point of view. As you will see, this relationship was doomed from the start because Jack had a very clear hidden agenda about which Teri knew nothing.

For whatever it's worth, Jack has a history of commitment-related problems. He was consistently unfaithful to his first wife and left her for another woman, who he did not marry. His second marriage was brief, with Jack once again leaving his wife for another woman. He eventually did marry this woman because she became pregnant.

Here's Jack's version of what happened with Teri:

"I liked Teri. We had a lot of fun on our first date. I asked her out for the next night. We went to dinner on a Friday night. I took her home, and I remember that I called her the next day and asked if she wanted to see a movie with me that night. She said, 'Great.' We had a lot of dates, four or five nights in a row. I was very attracted to her at first.

"The first time we slept together, she stayed over. After that I guess I didn't want her around. Sometimes I just felt pressured by her—I thought she would want something more. Sometimes it really was because the kids were going to call me or something was going on. I have a hard time dealing with a woman when the children are around because my dealings with the children often involve their mother.

"My ex-wife and I have sort of an odd relationship . . . some people wouldn't understand it . . . We still sleep together. It works out better this way. When we were living together, she was never interested in sex. Now we see each other often, and we sleep together maybe once every ten days or so. How could I tell Teri that?

"When Teri spent the night, I would want her to leave by eight in case my wife or the kids called—I never told my wife I was seeing other women, and she would have a jealous fit if she found out. What I usually did was tell Teri that the kids were coming over. She said that it felt as though the kids were getting dropped off earlier and earlier. I never stayed at her house because I worried about my wife calling and my not being home if she called in the middle of the night, which she does sometimes.

"Anyway, with Teri this pattern developed where I was less and less available. One night she invited me to her house for dinner; her roommate was away, and it was apparent she expected me to stay over. She sensed that I wasn't going to, and she said, 'You're not going to stay, are you?' I said, 'No,' and she said, 'I'm furious, I'm really angry . . . it's not your fault, but I'm really furious, so why don't you leave now?'

"I did, and then when I got home I wrote her this long letter. I told her that she deserved more than I was giving her. She's a lovely person and I didn't want to hurt her. She got the letter and suggested dinner to talk about it.

"We went to dinner, and she said that I shouldn't have slept with her. If I hadn't we could have been friends, but now she didn't want me as a friend. She said she had enough friends, and she indicated that, as I thought, she wanted a permanent relationship.

"I suspect the overriding reason the relationship didn't work out was because of what was going on with my wife. If it hadn't been for that, if I had met Teri at another time, it might have been different. That's what women always say to me: They always tell me that they wish they had met me at another time, when I was more emotionally available. I think they would like to analyze me, but I never see anyone long enough for them to take that latitude.

"In my emotional life, I often seem to have two women, neither one of whom is totally satisfying. When I left my first wife, it was for another woman; same thing with wife number two. Now with wife number three we're not together, but we are, and I see other women.

"Another reason things didn't work with Teri is that I don't really like blondes. I prefer women with dark hair. I was attracted to her to start out with—she was very feminine—but she wasn't really my type. However, as I say this, I realize that if it weren't for my wife, if I had met Teri in a vacuum, she might be very attractive to me.

"There was another problem with Teri, though, and this really bothered me. She was too affectionate . . . she touched me all the time. Not at the beginning, but at the end. I felt as though the touching was ever-present. If I moved to another seat, she moved with me . . . I couldn't go anywhere without her being right there. She was too clutchy. If it weren't for my wife, and I thought there was a reason to work on the relationship, I might have said something about it, but it didn't make sense to make her crazy by saying anything."

WHAT TERI SHOULD HAVE NOTICED

It's always easy in hindsight to say that there are certain things you should have noticed or shouldn't have put up with, but when a man is operating with a hidden agenda, it's not always as easy as it seems. Most women worry about appearing aggressive, pushy, dominating, and downright nosy. So they accept what they are told and don't probe. However, when a man is operating with a hidden agenda, he usually lets certain things leak out because, in a way, he wants you to know that other things are operating in his life. If you want to take care of yourself in relationships, you have to pay attention and assume responsibility for trying to find out what's really going on. Don't worry about being nosy—it's your life and your emotions, and you have to protect yourself. You are your first priority.

Let's take Jack's messages to Teri:

1. He told her about three marriages. Although there can certainly be reasons for this, in Jack's case, the fact that he indicated he had guilt about at least one of them should have clued Teri that perhaps he had reasons for the guilt. Jack's history

clearly indicates that he has a pattern of pitting women against each other. Teri should have noticed this.

2. He told Teri that his ex-wife was still jealous. Instead of assuming that Jack was the beleaguered party, Teri should have considered the possibility that if his ex-wife was jealous, she might still have some form of justifiable claim on Jack.

3. Jack had been separated from his wife for three years. One expects a recently separated man to be overly concerned with how his children view his social life, but after three years, Jack's attitude indicates that he wasn't being entirely honest about why the children were so "strange" about Teri and her phone call. The fact that he didn't want the children to know of her existence indicates a problem that is not entirely psychological.

4. Jack had time boundaries that existed from the very first. He made it clear to Teri that some days belonged to his children; he saw her on others. These kinds of rigid time restrictions tend to indicate a man who has "separate lives" and doesn't want anyone to have access to all of them. Moreover, in supposedly single, unattached men, these boundaries often indicate that another woman is making demands on the man's time.

HOW TERI WAS RESPONSIBLE FOR GOING ALONG WITH JACK'S HIDDEN AGENDA

Teri did what women often do: She assumed that the ex-wife was difficult and out of line. She was quick to believe that she, Teri, was somehow saner or more appropriate than the ex-wife. Jack conveyed that his ex-wife had problems loving him, and Teri accepted his explanation. She felt sorry for Jack because he had been married to such an impossible woman who was taking advantage of his good nature. Jack encouraged this.

When Teri first met Jack, he talked openly about his wives, his problems with them, his problems with his children. Teri didn't really listen. She paid attention to his pursuit, heard what she wanted to hear, and assumed he would be different with her, because she was "different."

If a man has a tendency to want to maintain the kind of unfair advantage a hidden agenda gives him, you can often spot it in what he tells you about previous relationships. Some questions to ask yourself before you get involved: How did he leave past relationships? Does he have a history of pitting women against each other? Is there an admitted history of dishonesty with another woman?

You can also get clues from the way he schedules time. When a man has a need for peculiar time boundaries, it is often because there is another woman making demands on his time. And something that every woman should understand: *If another woman is making demands on his time, it is because the man has somehow encouraged and allowed it.*

Chapter 5

SO CLOSE TO LOVE: WHEN HE'S IN TOO DEEP, AND HE KNOWS IT

Avoiding "hand in hand together" is what commitmentphobia is all about. Why? Because to these men such a structure implies an expectation of permanency, the one condition in life they cannot face. Yet these men do get involved in relationships. They even marry. So what happens when the commitmentphobic finds himself in a structured relationship? To understand his reactions, you have to think about what a permanent relationship means.

For the average man, a relationship with a member of the opposite sex can be a comfortable, as well as deeply rewarding, experience. But an ongoing relationship implies certain obligations, responsibilities, expectations, and (there's that word again) commitments. By definition, a relationship has a structure. Remember, to the hard-core commitmentphobic, any structure, no matter how loose, evokes anxiety and discomfort.

When one of these men begins to perceive his relationship as a confining structure, all of his fight or flight phobic reactions are triggered. Suddenly, what was once seen as a warm and loving haven is now regarded as a prison. And for no logical reason, he worries that he will be trapped inside forever.

MAINTAINING DISTANCE—THE COMMITMENTPHOBIC'S GOAL

You recognize the scenario: He couldn't rest until he knew he had you. Now you are there for him all the time. You may be living together, you may be married, or you may simply be so emotionally committed to him that you might as well be his wife.

YOUR GOAL: to work on the relationship, to solidify it and make it grow.

HIS GOAL: to find space or distance within the relationship.

How hard and far he looks for that space is dependent upon the degree of his phobic problem. A man with a mild anxiety response might be satisfied to do one of the following: come home late a few nights a week; develop hobbies that by definition exclude the woman; disappear into a different room in an attempt to gain space, etc.

A more serious commitmentphobic will distance himself even further, and may do one of the following: stay at work until all hours, or become proficient at a sport or hobby that legitimately keeps him away for days at a time.

The extreme commitmentphobic has an intense sense of being trapped and will choose extreme and intense methods of finding distance. He may do the following: be argumentative and abusive; refuse to be reliable or to be counted on; use other women as a way of creating and maintaining distance.

THE COMMITTED RELATIONSHIP—A CLAUSTROPHOBIC ENVIRONMENT

Remember, these men regard commitment, particularly marriage, as the ultimate trap. If you want to know how strongly many of them feel on the subject, imagine what it would be like to be trapped behind a brick wall—forever.

In the same way that a claustrophobic will not enter a room unless he knows there are readily accessible windows and doors, a commitmentphobic will not enter a relationship unless he knows he can find a way out. If you keep the image of the brick wall in mind, it will help you understand how much this man does not want to feel that he is stuck anywhere forever.

HOW A COMMITMENTPHOBIC KEEPS THE RELATIONSHIP INTACT . . . WHILE MAINTAINING HIS DISTANCE.

Some commitmentphobics are able to deal with their problem in a constructive fashion. This is typically seen in marriages in which distance and space are an accepted part of the implicit or explicit agreement between the couple.

A good example of this kind of marriage is the one that my friends Don and Joan have. I've known Don, a thirty-eight-year-old project engineer, for a long time. Until he met and married Joan, he never went out with anyone for more than six months. As a matter of fact, I didn't think he would ever marry, and he made many women unhappy by following a typical commitmentphobic pattern. With Joan it was immediately different. Her occupation—she was a sleep therapist involved in research—makes her unavailable many nights and most weekends (she actually sleeps in the lab many nights). She also travels a great deal, lecturing and teaching. Don has more free time and a less restricted schedule as a married man than he ever did as a single one. Sometimes he complains good-humoredly about Joan's work, but basically it seems to suit his needs.

Another type of relationship in which a commitmentphobic can be comfortable is seen in the kind of marriage in which the man works odd hours and rarely comes home, or buries himself in hobbies and outside interests.

A typical example is Bob, who admits to being both a claustrophobic and a commitmentphobic. He is also a jock. In the winter he plays squash and watches football games. In the spring and summer, he plays tennis and watches baseball. Every weekend of the year, he is involved in some athletic activity or another. His wife, who has her own interests, has no desire to join him, but as soon as his son was old enough, he took him wherever he went. Then he started coaching a Little League team. If you spend an evening with Bob and his wife, it is apparent that togetherness is not their thing. Although both of them say that they have a very satisfying and fulfilling marriage, they are rarely in the same room at the same time.

WHEN A COMMITMENTPHOBIC FEELS TRAPPED FOREVER

And then there are the worst-case commitmentphobics, the men who get into a committed relationship, or a marriage, and wake up one day feeling totally trapped. When such a man panics, he can see no way out of his dilemma without destroying the relationship. This man is unable to make a decision to leave a relationship and do it gracefully.

To complicate matters, he is not even always sure that he *wants* to leave. He just wants to know that the relationship is sufficiently miserable that he *can* leave at any time, should he want to, without much explanation. This man is so perverse that he is happiest when the relationship is in a shambles because then not only does he have a good reason for leaving, he can blame it on the woman.

I realize that most of us are told that there are always two sides to every story, but when a worst-case commitmentphobic is trying to make sure he is not trapped, he has to take a lion's share of the responsibility for sabotaging and destroying the possibility of love.

This man absolutely does not want the relationship to work. He absolutely thinks he may be stuck forever, and he is so panicked that he is incapable of finding a rational solution to his distress.

Like the claustrophobic stuck in an elevator, he truly perceives himself as being trapped forever behind a brick wall. Too out of control to find a door in the brick wall or to open it even when he sees it, this man figuratively begins to claw at the brick wall, tearing it down, and taking the real relationship along with it. A woman who is involved with such a man had better learn how to duck, because more often than not, he begins to throw these symbolic bricks one by one at the woman he perceives as his captor.

Such a man is rarely rational. All he knows is that he is feeling acute discomfort, which he probably cannot understand or discuss. When this man is involved, everything that happens between the couple revolves around his trapped feelings and what he does about them. How the relationship progresses or falls apart, the children, the sex, the fighting, the building, the destroying—all revolve around his need.

However, because he also needs the security of a woman's love, his conflict is enormous. When the woman gets fed up and withdraws, he often reverts to his pursuit/panic tactics, chases her down, and the whole process begins again. These men play a constant cat-and-mouse game with commitment, and any woman who gets involved with one of them is bound to suffer an amazing amount of pain.

Typically, a man such as this may begin belittling and emotionally abusing the wife-figure, or he may try to escape by finding women with whom he can have affairs. Whether you are the wife-figure or the other woman, unless you are prepared to take tolerance to the outer limits, or he changes drastically, you don't have a fighting chance.

THE HUSBAND AS FAULT FINDER: WHEN HIS "I DO" MEANS "I DON'T"

Some men are able to go through all of the stages up to and including the wedding ceremony before they hit the panic button. Typically this late bloomer starts to realize what is happening a day or so before the wedding, but total panic doesn't kick in until after the event.

When this happens, it is excruciatingly painful for the woman. Think about it. She marries a man who loves her, and she ends up with a man who acts as though he hates her. This is the man who is most often mistaken for a misogynist, the man who hates women. From my vantage point, although the woman's experience may be the same, the reasons for the man's behavior are quite different. The commitmentphobic doesn't hate his wife— he hates the marriage trap. He needs to know that he has a built-in excuse for ending the relationship if one day he wakes up and can't stand it anymore. So he starts looking for reasons why his wife is wrong for him and why the marriage won't work. He sabotages the relationship, usually from Day One.

All of the men I spoke to about this admitted feeling some guilt after the fact, but most of them say that all the while they are fault-finding, they are feeling mostly anger and resentment at being trapped with this woman. Several also said that when the woman goes out of her way to be particularly nice, or to smooth over such fault-finding, they think that she is being manipulative and is simply trying to tighten the trap.

Vince, who has been married and divorced twice, clearly recalls that with his first wife he was always trying to set the stage for getting out. He wanted to know that the arguments and reasons for leaving were always there:

"I knew I wanted to leave within weeks of getting married, but I didn't know how I was going to do it. Obviously I couldn't walk away if it was a successful marriage, so when things were going well between us, instead of being happy, I would start worrying that I wouldn't be able to get out . . . I would get furious at her and blame her for making me marry her. I would start fights with her. I know a relationship has to grow, but I didn't want it to grow with her. I started thinking that there was somebody out there who was better for me. The minute I start thinking that I might have to be with a particular woman forever, I immediately become aware of the fact that the woman isn't perfect. I know this is ridiculous. I know nobody's perfect, least of all me—but it's what I feel."

Women often ask whether or not a man feels guilty when he is being totally destructive to a woman. Vince says that at the time he was doing it, he felt guilty about wasting his wife's time—she could have gone out and married someone else and had the children she wanted. But he didn't feel guilt about hurting her ego or destroying her self-image:

"I said some awful things to my first wife. I feel guilty about it now, but while I was doing it, I had no idea how much damage I was doing to her ego. My reactions were almost instinctual. I felt as though I was suffocating in the marriage, and it was so necessary for my survival to act this way that I didn't even think about what I was doing to her as I did it. I just wanted to make sure that I had all the reasons I needed to get out, if I wanted to get out."

Several men have also told me that part of their reason for constant bickering was that they thought that perhaps the woman would be so unhappy that she might take the initiative and end the relationship so that they didn't have to be totally responsible for the breakup. Vince agrees with this:

"There's no question that I was also testing her—a part of me hoping that she would get disgusted and kick me out, another part terrified that this was going to happen. I remember my wife saying, 'If you find all these things wrong with me, why do you stay with me?' And I didn't have the guts to tell her that a large part of me didn't want to stay. Finally she left me."

USING ANOTHER WOMAN TO GET DISTANCE

If you're a man who wants to destroy a marriage, what better way to do so than to start an affair or a series of affairs? Typically the commitmentphobic is no different with these "other women" than he is with his wife . . . eventually. Usually he pursues one until she responds, then he feels just as trapped with her as he does with his wife, and he backs off.

So many women become involved with men who tell them they love them and that they plan to leave their wives. If you are the other woman, it's important to recognize that to the out-of-control commitmentphobic, you represent the open window and the way to get space, but only temporarily.

If you begin to care for him, if you begin to have expectations, if you ultimately want a commitment, he will be off and running, and you will no longer be part of his life. Instead, you will be history, and he will be off telling some third woman, or even his wife, how it was wrong, how it was stupid.

WHEN THE "OTHER WOMAN" MAKES HIM FEEL TRAPPED

Even though a man is married, he can still pursue a woman and go through all the phases of the pursuit/panic syndrome. This is clearly illustrated in the following story of an affair between a married man and a single woman.

KAREN: *Thirty-six, divorced ten years ago.*

Karen is the producer for a small theater in Colorado. She is a very articulate, thoughtful, and lovely woman who is struggling for insight and understanding. A woman who many men have found attractive, she is not someone who a married man would choose for a fling; she has too much depth and complexity. And yet David, a married man with three small children, went out of his way to involve her in his life.

This relationship, as you will see, had the kind of definite Beginning, Middle, and End that one expects when the man is unable to commit himself to any woman.

"In the beginning, David and I didn't have an affair. Every morning I would walk into town to get the paper. I always saw this man—David—and he looked very familiar. I saw him alone for several months. Then I saw him with a baby. I figured, 'married man with baby'—certainly safe to start a conversation here."

So Karen said hi to him, and it turned out that they had known each other, but not well, in college. As they parted on that first day, David handed Karen a business card, which she thought was pretentious and a bit weird.

"Soon after that, he started calling me on Mondays, the day the theater is closed. I was under a lot of pressure. It was a new theater, and I had put money and time into making it work, but it still wasn't happening. I couldn't always pay my overhead, and I was depressed, nervous, and scared. My whole life then was work, and on my day off, I would go to bed and hide, and he would call, and I would wonder, 'Why is this man calling me?' I couldn't remember anything about him except that he had this baby, he had been one of the least attractive men at school, and he had an angry look that disappeared when he spoke, but I couldn't see that on the phone. And he would say, 'What are you doing?' and I would say, 'I'm in bed,' and he would say, 'Are you alone?' So I thought not only was he ugly and pretentious, with an angry look, he was also gross. Then he would ask me to lunch, and I would say no. Sometimes he called several times a day, and I would find myself screaming, 'No.' I'm not abusive to men, but I was abusive to David. He would start trying to talk me out of my mood, and I would get guilty. After a few weeks of this, he didn't seem so awful, and besides, I thought it would be mentally healthy for me to get out."

I have to stop here to comment that an amazing number of women who got involved with men with commitment problems talked themselves into the first date on the grounds that they needed to get out more. I did not get the impression that these women were rationalizing; I think it is an honest reaction. I do think, however, that Karen's story points up in one more way how many women, in our society, still feel that they need a man to help them "get out."

Karen says she didn't know what David wanted from her, but she found herself going to lunch with him, and he would encourage her to talk about herself, which she did. She says that he listened attentively as though he cared.

"I decided that he was bored because he didn't work. By coincidence he was a playwright, who had never had a play produced. He had a little bit of money from some rentals on real estate back East that had come up in value. He would say things like, 'They'd have to pay me a lot of money to get me to work.' So I thought he was brilliant. Before I met David, I would believe anything a man told me. He told me he didn't choose to work so I assumed that this was an intelligent guy with all the powers that men have, and that he had made a choice. Wasn't that great. The rest of us work, work, work, work all the time, but here was someone who chose not to do this. It never entered my mind that he was afraid to work, or he felt inadequate to work, or that he had problems. Also, he appeared very calm, very much in control. He told me he was happily married, and all he wanted to talk about were my problems. I assumed they were his entertainment."

After about a year of lunches, David started inviting Karen to his house for lunch. She couldn't help but notice that his wife was never there. Sometimes she would be at her sister's with the kids. Sometimes she would just be away, and he would have the children. It appeared to Karen, as it would to many women, that he and his wife were never in the same place at the same time, and that his wife didn't seem to care what he did.

"Then one day, out of the blue, David began to talk about us giving each other massages, and it was as if for the first time, he was allowing me to see that he was attracted to me. I was confused by it and discussed it with my therapist. He openly encouraged me to have an affair. He said, 'Karen, you're on a desert and you are starving . . . somebody comes along and offers you a McDonald's, but you were dreaming of a steak dinner. Doesn't it make sense to take the McDonald's until you get to a steak dinner?' "

Karen says that the next time he talked about massage, they ended up in bed, in his place. She remembers thinking about the fact that it was his wife's bed, which seemed really strange. He didn't seem at all concerned by it, but she began to ask about his marriage.

"David never said anything negative about his wife, just that they didn't have sex anymore. He said that she complained that he was never loving to her and that he expected her to turn on just for sex, which she couldn't do. I asked him if he loved his wife, and he said that when they were first married his wife would always ask him if he loved her. He said he would always reply, 'I'm doing the best I can.'

"It became apparent to me that there were problems in David's marriage, but I thought it had to be his wife's fault. After all, from everything I had seen, the man was totally loving, supportive, and kind. I was feeling more optimistic about myself and my business, and the support and encouragement he had given me had been very instrumental in that. I was very grateful, and I wanted to do the same for him. I absolutely didn't want to break up his marriage. I had no obsession with him, and I placed no demands on him. If he called, fine. If he didn't, that was fine, also. Sex wasn't that great at first because I wasn't attracted to him, but I learned to love his loving me."

As time went on, David got more and more into Karen's life. If he was like many typical commitmentphobics—and there is no reason to suspect that he was not—the fact that Karen was an independent woman with her own business and no desire to break up his marriage gave him the sense that she didn't really need him. As she said, she had no long-range plans as far as David was concerned. Then he did what many commitment-phobics do—he began to play a moth–flame game with his life. Flirting with disaster, he encouraged her to make demands on him and to call him at home. At the time, Karen thought that he was just naive and that it would have been insane to threaten his marriage or his wife in that way.

After they had been sleeping together about nine months, Karen met another man and went out with him, on New Year's Day. She had been alone on New Year's Eve.

"David phoned while the man was in my apartment to wish me a happy new year, and he freaked when I said I had a date. I was genuinely shocked . . . I didn't think David and I were in love; I thought we were having an old-fashioned affair which he wanted more than I did.

"The following day, he came over to my office and started having an anxiety attack, a major anxiety attack. He told me that he loved me. 'But I love you,' he said. 'What do you mean?' I kept asking him. 'What do you mean you love me? You're living with your wife, you're sleeping with your wife.' Besides, what was the big deal? All I had was a date.

"He was hyperventilating and couldn't breathe. I had to sit him on a couch behind the theater. I was so frustrated. I was supposed to be working, and instead I was trying to calm a married man because I had had a date. It was ridiculous. But I began to believe him when he said I was important to him.

"I told David I would have to rethink the relationship, and

I did. I didn't realize before that he loved me. I knew I didn't love him, but he loved me. He was only the second man in my life who had told me he loved me, and he seemed very sincere. I decided that if he said I was that important to him, I was. So I told him that I wouldn't go out with anyone else. Myself I told that I would take any situation as it came up, but that if I found somebody I wanted to go out with, I certainly wasn't going to tell David unless I had to."

Karen and David continued like this until the summer, and she remembers him being consistently adoring. Then Karen decided to take a vacation. Once again, David had an anxiety attack.

"I realized the bizarre leverage I had over him was sex. He was afraid I would sleep with someone else. I said if he was so worried why didn't he come on vacation with me, and that's what he did. You have to understand that his wife made this all very easy. She went off to her parents' in the mountains every summer and accepted it when David said he hated the mountains. Since his wife wasn't accustomed to having him around in the summer, we agreed that she wouldn't miss him. At the time, I thought she was foolish for not choosing a vacation site that David would enjoy. Now, I realize he would have found fault with anything."

So Karen and David went off to California and drove along the coast. Karen remembers cheerfully stopping to help David choose gifts for his wife. Remember, she still wasn't thinking about anything permanent. That all changed in the airport on the way home; that's where David proposed.

"I told him I would think about it. And I did. I had been married before, and I didn't want to jump into anything, but I had begun to take David very seriously. Nothing had ever gone wrong between us. He was always loving, never cranky or moody, always accepting. We seemed to be able to talk out all our little differences, and I thought we had a very sweet love.

"Then, a day or so after our return, David suddenly went

into a complete panic and came to me crying. He thinks his wife is having an affair, and he is falling to pieces over it. I'm afraid I became enraged. I said, 'What? You just ran away to spend two weeks with me, you spent money on me that you should have spent on your wife and kids, you spent it on me, and now you're here whining to me that maybe your wife is having an affair? What's the matter with you? You tell your therapist about this, because I don't want to listen.' I was furious.

"He looked at me and whimpered, 'But you're my friend.'

" 'I'm your lover,' I said. 'Don't you understand that?'

"He didn't know what hit him, and he couldn't understand my reactions. So he went off to his wife, and cried and told her his fears, and she said, 'David, I love you too much to do anything like that.' He tells me this!"

This was a side of David that Karen had never seen before. It was so different from his facade that she says she thought it was a momentary aberration brought on by the stress of deciding to leave one woman and marry another. Now she says that she realizes it was a message, and she should have responded to the reality of what was happening, but it seemed so bizarre and incomprehensible. Also, he was continuing to give her another message: He was still talking about marriage.

"During that fall and winter, we mutually agreed that we would marry. All David had to do was leave his wife, and he said he wasn't sure when or how to do it. Sometimes I would press a little, and he would say, 'We have time, we have the rest of our lives.' I figured he was being sensitive and thoughtful to his wife, and I could respect him for that, so I didn't want to press.

"There was one clear moment when I thought the relationship might not work out. David used to call me five or six times a day. It made it impossible to work, so I asked him please not to call me during the day. I knew intuitively, whether I had meant it that way or not, that I was making a demand for him to spend more time with me at night. As soon as I said it, I sensed that David was not going to do the things he said—but I attributed my feeling of pain and loss at that moment to an overdeveloped sense of drama."

Most women have told me that they have had such moments of clarity in relationships with men like David, and when they look back they see that it signified the beginning of the end. In this case, Karen's unspoken demand for prime time was probably the first demand she made of David, and it signified the beginning of a change in her attitude. She was no longer happy being David's girlfriend; she wanted marriage. She wanted a firm commitment, and she wanted him to leave his wife. This change in turn brought about a change in David's behavior.

"Then Memorial Day came round, and since it was on a Monday, I assumed we would spend it together, as we did every Monday. To start out with, I'm anxious about being alone on major holidays. In this case, it fell on "our" day. When David said he had to spend it with his wife and family, I got furious. I said something wonderfully classic like, 'But Monday is my day,' and threw a glass on the floor. It didn't even break. He got angry with me, and asked *me* how I could treat *him* this way. Once again, he said that we had the rest of our lives. This time, I pushed him out the door.

"Within hours he called from a phone booth. He felt terrible. I felt terrible. So we made up."

Karen was genuinely reluctant to push David, but she wanted this stage of the relationship to end—she wanted David to act on what he had been saying, but she was getting the feeling that he was not as strong as he appeared to be. Also, David was giving her permission to push him. He told her that his therapist said that if he stayed with his wife, he would be unhappy for the rest of his life and if he married Karen, he would go through some pain from the stress of leaving his wife, but he would ultimately be very happy. Karen felt convinced that David needed help in getting out of his marriage.

Her therapist said that some people need an ultimatum and suggested that as a method of getting David to move, but Karen was uncomfortable with manipulation so she discussed this with David himself.

"I told David what my therapist suggested and for a while we went back and forth on the subject of an ultimatum. Finally, at the end of June, I said, 'Okay, I'll give you three months.' "

In the meantime it had become apparent to Karen that David's wife was aware that something was happening. David would repeat conversations to her in which his wife said that it was apparent that the marriage wasn't working and asked whether he wanted a divorce. David's wife was unwittingly opening doors and giving David the sense that he was not really trapped in the marriage.

"When his wife asked what was going on, David would say he didn't want to discuss it. Finally he told me that she asked him if he was having an affair. He answered by saying, 'Who would stand for that?' Once again I got furious. I told him that he had twenty-four hours; he had to do something or we were finished.

"His wife was at her parents' summer place. When he left to go there, I thought I would probably never hear from him again, but I was okay. I was prepared to accept whatever happened. I imagined two possible scenarios: Either he had decided to stay with his wife and try to make the marriage work, or he had told his wife and was feeling some sadness, along with a sense of relief, and would be prepared to go forward with our life together.

"Well, neither scenario was correct. Instead David called and his tone sounded cold and angry and dead. 'Well,' he said, 'It was the worst thing I have ever had to do.' "

Everything about what he said and the way he said it made Karen feel as though she was a murderer. Suddenly it was *her* fault that his wife was hurt. He told Karen that he was planning to stay there for the weekend and that *maybe* he would call her when he got back. Karen couldn't help but pick up on the "maybe." Remember, this was a man she had to ask to please *not* call every hour. His whole attitude toward her was changing, and she didn't know what was going on.

"Well, he did call when he returned, and he had indeed

told his wife he was leaving, but he continued to live there with her and the kids. He said he couldn't live in my apartment—it was too small, even as a temporary solution. Also, he was totally different. Where once, nothing was too much for him to do to please me, suddenly everything was too much. Walking around the block with me became a chore rather than a blessing. Where once he had been all enthusiasm, love, and tenderness, now he was negative . . . about *everything*. This period lasted only a few days because I looked at David and thought, 'So this is the way he has always been with his wife.' "

David had yet to move in with Karen, but in his head, he had told his wife he was leaving, and although she was hurt, she had accepted it. He was now free to spend as much time at Karen's as he wanted. But somehow, Karen had ceased to be his joy and had become instead his captor. As far as Karen's feelings were concerned, there is no question that David's attitudinal change was making her insecure and clutchy.

"I suddenly knew I was in a lot of trouble with this guy. I told this to my therapist, who said, 'You *are* in a lot of trouble; you don't even know what kind of trouble you're in.' He suggested we see a couples counselor, and David, who was still paying lip service to our commitment to each other, agreed. I told the counselor that David said he was divorcing his wife and marrying me, but when it came to the nitty gritty, it didn't seem to be working out that way.

"On our way to the second session, just after he finished parking the car, David put his arms around me and told me that he loved me more than anything else in the world. At that time I was still convinced—David convinced me—that he would love me to the day he died, that nothing could dissuade him from loving me. Inside the session itself, it all became a blur, and I don't remember everything. I think I was talking about the fact that David didn't seem to *understand* that what was happening between us was causing me pain; he didn't seem at all upset by my distress. Then the therapist said, 'Don't you see, Karen, David doesn't care about your unhappiness. Isn't that right, David?' David just sat there and said that she was right. Even I had the sense to know that I was concerned with his unhappiness and pain and that something was dreadfully wrong. Then the counselor said, 'David can't make a commitment, isn't that right, David?' And again, David said yes, that it was right.

"So that was the end. It ended right there. All I could feel was shock and pain. It wasn't that I couldn't live without David. I could. It was the utter meaninglessness of everything he had ever said to me. It was a horrendous experience for me. I couldn't eat; I couldn't sleep. I ran into him a week later. He was fine—rosy-cheeked and fine. I had excruciating agony from the fact that he was totally unaffected. So I decided that David must be having a breakdown. Temporary insanity was the only explanation I could accept."

It is easy to see why Karen decided that her David had lost his mind. She didn't understand how any supposedly normal man could go through the kind of emotional upheaval she and David had experienced without looking upset. She was sure David hadn't been lying to her for what had now been several years. Who would go to so much trouble? It didn't make any sense, so she decided that he was in the middle of a breakdown. Once he recovered and realized what he had done, he would be back.

"In my heart, I decided he would be back. I just didn't want to believe that the love we had shared wasn't real. So I made it through the summer, but I lost twenty pounds. Then in September David called and asked if he could come over. Of course I said yes.

"He was exactly as he had been at the beginning. 'You are such a saint,' he said. 'Can you ever forgive me?' I thought he was back and the nightmare was over, so of course I could forgive him. It all started again. Same thing: We talked about marriage, and he made plans to leave his wife. And, same thing, he changed with me. The David who I had known, the man who had always tried, always listened, who said he always wanted to do anything he could to make me happy, didn't exist anymore. In his place was a man who didn't want to give—*anything*.

"I told him the way I was feeling, and he said, 'I'm doing the best I can.' He used the same words with me that he told me he had used when his wife asked him if he loved her. I thought about it: He hadn't even left her, and already he was treating me like he always treated her.

"Then a miracle happened. I was invited to a party on a Saturday night, and David didn't want to go. But another man called that afternoon, and I asked him to go with me. True to form, David went bananas. He became convinced, no matter what I said, that I would ask the man to spend the night with me, so he responded by deciding that he was definitely going to go home and tell his wife that he was leaving. I thought, 'Isn't it strange that the only way I can get this man to move is by threatening him. This is very strange to me and has nothing to do with love.' "

Although Karen was still involved, she had enough distance and experience with David to realize that she didn't have the strength or desire to have this kind of relationship. She was emotionally exhausted from his pursuit/panic syndrome.

"David showed up the next morning and said he had told his wife that he was having an affair. To me this did not sound like a man who wanted to leave his wife; it sounded like a man who wanted to create chaos in the lives of everyone around him. Later in the day I went to my therapist, who agreed. He said, 'Look, Karen, a man who wants to get out of a relationship doesn't want more problems or discussions, he just wants to get out. Now his wife won't let him out of her sight.'

"When I got home that afternoon, David phoned. I told him what my therapist had said. 'You're right,' he said. 'Everything has changed,' he said. I felt my heart go thump, thump, thump. 'I love my wife,' he said.

"I asked him to come over, and to my amazement he agreed. When he walked through the door I hit him. I continued to hit him for forty-five minutes. I couldn't believe he let me. When I finally stopped, he said the most outrageous things. He told me that he couldn't remember if he had ever loved me, but he knew he certainly no longer felt anything for me, and he *really* loved his wife. He kept repeating that he was a married man, as though I hadn't understood that to start out with. He told me that he didn't want me calling him at home anymore. I had not called him before, and I certainly had no intention of doing so now. As a matter of fact, I never spoke to David again.

"During our last year together, I had worked with David on the play he was writing, and I promised him that we would produce it if he finished it. He did, and I followed through on my promise, although my assistant handled all the details. Later, I discovered that he had asked out a woman that he had met at the theater a year before."

When her relationship with David began, Karen believed that David's problem was that he was in a boring marriage with a wife who was not satisfying his needs. By the time it ended, she knew that this was not the case.

"My sin in my relationship with David was one of pride, hubris. I had so much ego; I assumed that I was the heroine. I thought I was different from his wife; somehow I was better. At the end, I was exactly the same as his wife, asking, 'Do you love me, do you love me?' David still replying, 'I'm doing the best I can.' I thought we had a real love, a sweet love. I thought three years of love wouldn't go away so quickly. I was wrong. But I think David was very unfair. I think he knew the truth about himself. I didn't, but he did."

WHAT ABOUT THE WIFE?

If you are the other woman, it's easy to have a peculiar notion about what sort of woman the man you love is married to. He says she doesn't care what he does, and you may believe him. He says she has her own life, and you may think that life includes other men. He says, "We've never really gotten along," and you assume it's her fault. More often than not, the wife is just a woman trying to have an honest relationship with the same man.

JOYCE: Forty, mother of five children—including one set of twins—ages ten to eighteen.

Joyce is a good example of the sort of woman who is married and plans to stay married to her commitmentphobic husband. She has pretty much adjusted to Hal's need for distance and has even learned to adjust to his frequent affairs. Another woman might become enraged or leave. Originally she stayed for the sake of the children; now she stays because it has gotten easier with time. She says that financial considerations have something to do with her decisions. I think she genuinely loves her husband, and she is an unusually strong and determined woman.

Joyce is a glamorous, sophisticated, elegant, and well-traveled New Yorker. But this wasn't always the case. Nineteen years ago, when she married her husband, she was a naive and protected girl from rural Vermont.

"I realize now Hal wouldn't have married me if it hadn't been for the Vietnam War. We had been going out—maybe once a week—for over a year. He was not the only boy I was dating, but he was certainly the most appealing to me. He didn't have any money at all, and his head was always in the clouds, but I was *really* attracted to him. He had this very intense look, and he seemed to need me even if he never showed it. Even then, I have to admit, he was not one hundred percent reliable about calling or showing up when he said he would. But, you know, I was so popular and independent, it didn't even occur to me that a time might come when this might bother me. Also, even though we went to the same college, we didn't see that much of each other. My roommate was dating his roommate. They were really hot and heavy, and I think that we were brought together socially by them a lot more than we might have if it was left to him. At that time, most people thought of him as sort of a goof-off, and reckless and careless. I might have thought that, too, if I had known him better. In any event, he was graduating and he got his draft notice, so he asked me to marry him. He didn't so much as say, 'Let's get married, so I won't have to go to Vietnam,' but in retrospect that's probably what he was thinking. Then, I just thought he didn't want to be separated from me.

"Anyway, he asked me to go away with him for a weekend, and I said I couldn't do that. So he said, 'Well, then let's get married.' I said, 'Okay.' It takes some people longer to order their dinner in a restaurant than it took me to make my decision. I think I wanted to go to bed with him, but I didn't know how to do it without getting married. I was still young. I'd had a strict and religious upbringing, and although I had friends who had slept with their boyfriends, it seemed forbidden to me. In any event, when he proposed it was around midnight on a Saturday night. We called my parents and then his parents. We ran around the following week getting a license, a ring, planning a small ceremony. My parents came in for it, and we were married a week later, the next Saturday."

Making a commitment to avoid a commitment may seem strange, but I've discovered that many commitmentphobic men do just that. Often they marry one woman in order to avoid another; in this case, Hal's marriage gave him a reason not to go into the army. Another quality that's often present when these men get married is speed. Often they get married in a way that leaves little time to back out. When they stop to think about it after the fact, the marriage has an almost accidental quality.

"Well, we went off for our honeymoon, and we got along really well sexually, as I knew we would. Then Hal got a job in Chicago, and we moved there. We found this tiny little apartment and he went off to work every day. True to form, I got pregnant on my honeymoon. In the meantime, he was working really long hours. He complained constantly about his job, but he always seemed to want to be there. I rarely saw him. He was doing research on this drug and he practically lived in the lab, or with the people he worked with. After the baby was born, I got accustomed to being alone. Then he went back to business school nights, so I was alone even more. And, of course, I got pregnant again. I was quite isolated from friends and other people like us for two reasons: We were living in a low rent district, and people my age had stopped getting married and getting pregnant. I would talk to my friends, and they were all off in nifty apartments finding careers. When I asked Hal to spend more time at home, he looked at me as though I was being outrageous. Maybe he spent one night a week at home. Maybe. My kids became my best buddies.

"In the meantime, Hal began shifting jobs. He got a job working for this vitamin company, selling to stores, which was a real change in direction for him. Now he traveled on the job, so he would be away for whole days at a time. Sex was always good, and when he came home, he seemed happy with the marriage. I was the one who was miserable. My whole life revolved around the kids. I had them less than two years apart and they kept me busy. I probably would have left him, but I didn't know where to go. My parents would never have understood, and I felt so isolated from everyone by my situation. There I was, little Mrs. Susie Q. Housekeeper. It was embarrassing to admit that my husband never, ever came home.

"Then, after we were married about eight years, two things happened. We got rich, and I discovered that Hal was having affairs. Hal put his chemistry background together with his sales and marketing skills and put together a line of natural cosmetics and similar products. He made a fortune. We should have been happy. Finally, he didn't have to work as hard. He didn't have to be out every night. But it got worse. He just didn't know how to stay home, so he started having affairs. He may have had them before, but I never found out about them. In any event, at first, when I just suspected other women, I did odd things. I left the toilet seats up all the time and put crumpled cigarettes in our ashtrays (I don't smoke) so he might think a man had been there. We had a few terrible fights. I did everything I could think of. I wheedled and cajoled, and he promised to change and didn't. I became more and more depressed. It was so bad sometimes that I could barely get out of bed. Finally, one of his affairs seemed serious, so I left. I packed up the kids and left. It was summer, so it was easy because the kids weren't in school. I took them to the country. He came after us, but he couldn't find us for days. Finally my brother told him where we were.

"I'll never forget that day. He came into the kitchen. When he looked out the window and saw my youngest daughter on a swing in the backyard, he started to cry. I was amazed; I just couldn't believe it. This was the first indication I ever had that he had any sensitivity other than just being distant, cold, and standoffish. I knew that we had a fairly good sexual relationship, but it was only that. So my feeling was that sex was my only route to get through whatever shell he had built around himself. Nothing else. He wasn't good at communicating with me any other way. I thought he had no real feelings. But that day, he looked so upset. I felt so bad. I'm not one to give up easily so I decided to go back. I don't think it was an act that day in the country. Did he really change after that? No, but at least I believed he wanted to, and at least I felt a little more sorry for him because he doesn't mean to be as self-centered and inconsiderate as he is.

"Every time I want to leave, I remember that day in the country. I guess I decided that it was better for my children to have a father whenever they had one than to have none at all, and that if I was going to stay with him, I had to find more of a life for myself. It got easier because the kids got older, and we got richer. Now I have a very good life. I take trips. I do whatever I want; he never begrudges me anything. I've never had any real desire to have affairs or anything—my upbringing may be too old-fashioned for that. But I love tennis and museums and restaurants and the theater. I can do pretty much anything I want. I have a good relationship with my kids, and I have a lot of friends.

"I realize he can't take too much of being with the family. On holidays, he's always the one who insists on the big traditional family day. Then after he's got us all assembled, he goes into the other room by himself, closes the door, and reads the paper. He wants to know that we are there for him if he wants us, but he gets nervous when he's around us very much. I know it's insane, but that's the way he is, and he's my husband."

THE COMMITMENTPHOBIC HUSBAND

What about the commitmentphobic husband? What kind of man is it who can make women so unhappy?

Perhaps the most amazing thing about the commitmentphobic husband is the extremes to which he goes in order not to feel trapped. His discomfort is often so great that he loses sight of the fact that his wife is a human being. When he fell in love with her, he may have been acutely aware of the kind of person she was. Yet, after marriage, he is often so intensely uncomfortable, so anxious, and so out of control that he can no longer see her clearly. He is often a man without mercy. His anxiety to find space and freedom within a relationship in which he feels trapped is no less terrifying to watch than that of the recently captured animal. He is flailing, and it will do no good to point out to him that his wife is just a woman and that she probably loves him. He can no longer see the reality of the situation. In his head she is his captor.

MARRIAGE DOES NOT MAKE A COMMITMENTPHOBIC SETTLE DOWN

When women get involved with a man who has commitment difficulties they think that something magical is going to happen once they are married. They hope marriage will make the man settle down. If anything, marriage often has the exact opposite effect. A man who feels trapped, closed in, or suffocated does not want to settle down; he wants to break free. When a man feels trapped, closed in, or suffocated, he simply doesn't see clearly, and his behavior toward his wife, or the woman who is making him feel trapped, is genuinely outrageous.

Here are some of the more common ways in which a commitmentphobic might behave:

■ He pretends he's not in a committed relationship.

I heard of one married man who told everyone that he was single (he had been married for years) until the day his wife got a divorce. Only then did he begin talking about his wife, to the shock and amazement of many of his friends. Granted, this man is rather an extreme case, but many commitmentphobics do a variation of this. Many men, particularly when they are traveling, pretend that they are not married. Many others, in longterm relationships, don't allow the woman involved to share in certain areas of their lives—in these areas, the man probably doesn't tell people that he has a steady girlfriend.

This behavior is obviously very painful to the woman, who feels excluded and left out.

■ He acts as if his wife is his jailer, and rarely has a kind word for her.

Many commitmentphobics feel that they are trapped in a relationship because they genuinely love the woman. This often makes them angry at the woman. They may irrationally feel that somehow she did something that put them in this extraordinarily uncomfortable position. These men rarely have any mercy for the woman and can be unrelentingly unkind.

When this happens, women usually don't know what is going on; all they can be sure of is that the man alternates between excessive protestations of love and disgusting displays of anger.

■ He finds a sense of freedom by using other women to act out his problems.

Infidelity is, obviously, the easiest way for a man to convince himself that he really isn't trapped by his marriage. It is interesting to note that many commitmentphobics who are amazingly unfaithful when they are married calm down when they are single.

This, of course, is not much consolation for the woman who is married to or seriously involved with one of these men.

> **ROBERT:** *A divorced forty-one-year-old English professor with three children.*

Robert's marriage lasted almost ten years. During that time, he used just about every commitmentphobic technique to distance himself from his wife. He is a good example of a man who wanted, and needed, to get out so badly that he couldn't even find the door until he had totally demoralized his wife. Robert is a sensitive man, an English professor. He is aware of people, their moods, and their needs. He also likes women. He liked the young woman he married, when he married her. She certainly had not done anything cruel or outlandish to him—other than marrying him.

Robert was in his early twenties when he married and his wife was already pregnant. Robert, who is very honest as well as articulate about his problems, knew even then that he was less than ecstatic about the notion of commitment.

"We had been living together off and on for about four years when Beth got pregnant. She wanted the baby, and I was too young and unsure of myself to stop her. I was very ambivalent about becoming a father and terrified of it. However, I assisted at the baby's birth, and I loved the child. I guess I got married out of a sense of duty.

"I remember the day after our marriage, the first time I introduced Beth as my wife, I felt a sense of doom. I didn't want it. I felt as though I had walked into a small dark room, a black box I didn't like. Even though I loved my wife at the time, and the baby, at least half of me felt trapped and boxed."

Beth was Robert's first real lover, and he was faithful until after they got married. Several of the men I have interviewed have mentioned a similar sexual pattern—they were faithful until marriage and excessively unfaithful while married. In the case of Robert and Beth, they were married less than six months when he had his first affair. It lasted about a week.

"Then I started to sleep with other women on a regular basis. My work kept me out nights, and I used it as an excuse, a cover to never come home. Commitment and marriage changed the nature of the relationship; I got resentful because of Beth's dependency. The more resentful I got, the more insecure and clinging she got. It became a vicious cycle."

I have found that women who are married to men who are being extremely destructive often resort to a childlike dependent attitude. It's as though they feel that if they were to act like an adult, they would have to automatically walk away from the relationship. Several have told me that they get "clingy" in the hope that the man will become protective. They think they are appealing to the man's better nature. This rarely, if ever, works.

In Robert's case, this problem was compounded because he admittedly also felt dependent on his wife; he didn't want her to leave or throw him out, so he didn't give her a completely honest message about what he was doing and the way he felt.

"I didn't want my marriage to end because I was also dependent on her. I didn't tell her about the other women, but I would leave clues, and she would find out. Then she didn't know how to handle it, so she would alternate between getting furious and trying to look the other way. I would alternate between denying what I was doing and setting things up so she would find out.

"From time to time, we were on the verge of breaking up. Right before our third child was born, we almost did it. I went so far as to get another place to live. I treated the marriage as though it was a rubber band, and I wanted to stretch this rubber band of a relationship, to distance myself as far as I could without actually leaving; to express my anger without leaving. Then we both got frightened and got back together . . . We were like two frightened people clinging to the same leaky raft for support."

Robert would be the first to admit that his behavior wore down his wife's self-esteem. His discomfort was so great that he couldn't stop himself from lashing out at the woman he married, the woman who he perceived as responsible for his plight.

"She kept trying to adjust and accommodate. No woman could have done this, so we fought a lot. She resented my always looking at other women. Her jealousy was well-founded because I literally slept with dozens of them. I couldn't stop resenting her dependency, although I don't know what I expected a young woman with young children to do. I said and did horrible things to her. I was the more articulate, the more sure of myself in the world, and I would pick her apart in a base, petty parody of intellectual debate.

"For the most part, she wanted the marriage to continue and I wanted it to end. I was with women all the time. But for years, whenever we got close to breaking up, I would get upset and think that I needed her. I even cried.

"But we never really talked out the problems. I think we were both afraid to. She would ask me to just be home before dawn, and I would go out with other women and come home after dawn. We would fight, and I would apologize. I would say that I would change. But I didn't know what that meant. I didn't know how to change. I figured it meant that I would somehow prevent myself from doing what I wanted to do.

"When we finally decided to split, we were just both exhausted from years of this insane marriage. The motif was weariness, and we agreed that I would find a place to live. It took a couple of weeks. It's interesting that our sexual relationship improved tremendously during that two-week period when we had finally decided to separate. I don't remember the actual ending. The hardest part, of course, was telling the children.

"At first after I left I was very ambivalent. I was frightened, but I also had an amazing sense of freedom. I remember feeling I had escaped something. It was like being let out of a cage. I was glad I didn't have to answer to my wife anymore. I was glad I didn't have to come home. Then, a few weeks later, once more I had a change of heart. I got depressed, and I tried to get my foot back in the door of my marriage. I said things like, 'Maybe we can get back together, and maybe we should think about seeing each other.' Fortunately, my wife would have none of it.

"I've always had a need to wander, not just sexually, but in every way. I tend to need job change, location change. I move a lot. I don't like the sense of being pinned down in one spot. Instead of making me settle down, marriage intensified these needs."

THE COMMITMENTPHOBIC AND HIS CHILDREN

One might expect the commitmentphobic to be just as unreliable with his children as he is with women. Interestingly, this does not appear to be the case. Although most of the men interviewed admitted to being terrified at the prospect of having children, those who had already become fathers were no less involved than non-commitmentphobic parents. As a matter of fact, in some cases, they appeared to be exceptionally devoted and involved with their children. As they see it, children grow up and go away . . . wives don't.

Chapter 6

WHEN HE CAN'T LOVE

<u>PHILIP:</u> *A forty-three-year-old photographer—single.*

If I were to point to a classic example of a commitmentphobic man, it would probably be someone like Philip. As far as women are concerned, not only has he never been able to form a permanent attachment, but he has pursued and rejected scores of them, most of whom he describes as being "all wrong" for him.

Philip's personal history is filled with examples of the many variations on the commitmentphobic theme, with one exception: He has never had any maritally induced commitmentphobia because he has never married. However, like many of these men, he is intensely attracted to the notion of a permanent commitment and is sincerely disappointed that he doesn't have one in his life. Yet he seems powerless to change either what he does or the women with whom he does it. I think one of the reasons he agreed to talk to me was that he has reached a point in his life where he is truly frustrated by his inability to commit. In the course of our conversations, he said that if I had approached him two years ago, he would have had neither the ability nor the desire to talk about this openly. He's mature enough to know that he can no longer blame others; he knows that he has orchestrated both the rise and fall of the majority of his relationships. While talking to him, I sensed that this was a painful subject for him, and he was obviously deeply troubled by much of his personal history.

A forty-three-year-old highly acclaimed photographer, Philip spends most of the year in Boulder, Colorado. The rest of the time he could be on location any place in the world. Articulate, attractive, intelligent, sensitive, and successful, Philip appears to be the kind of man young women dream about when they dream about love. Philip is aware that he is attractive to women. He thinks it is because he is sympathetic to women and likes to talk about many of the same things they do, such as feelings and relationships. His whole attitude is very appealing, but for a woman who is unprepared, getting involved with him could turn out to be a nightmare.

Philip has been engaged twice, but he has never married. His longest relationship lasted less than four years and ended badly. He is confused and genuinely distressed by his relationship failures. He has no desire or intention to cause anyone pain and has spent a lot of time trying to understand why he always walks away from commitment. By his own admission, he has copped out too many times, and there is little about his history with women that could be judged reasonable.

"I've gone out with too many women, slept with too many women, disappointed too many women. A couple of years ago, I dated one woman who was embarrassed to tell me that she had been married four times. At first I was shocked, but when I thought about it, I had to acknowledge that at least she had tried. Think about it. She had only had four relationships in fifteen years, and she had tried to make each of them work. I've had hundreds that I haven't tried at, and I can't remember many of the women's names."

Like many commitmentphobics, Philip idealizes marriage. It is something he wants, but he can't really imagine what it means.

"I have a fantasy vision of my life in the future. I see myself as a happily married grandfather who is quietly, peacefully, enjoying life. The reality: I don't have the slightest idea how I can get there.

"I don't have the richness and quality in my life that I think I should. I used to think that I would be a real good partner, but I'm beginning to wonder if it is ever going to happen. As much as I may talk about it, I recognize my inability to zero in on the right kind of person and to commit myself to the right situation.

"I choose women who fall all over me, because I like it at the beginning. Then I ultimately am irritated by it and walk away. I choose women who don't have real work, who are overly dependent, and I want a woman who stands on her own, who is capable of making decisions I'll respect."

Philip's aversion to commitment extends into several areas of his life. He does not, for example, ever write in pen in his date book. As a matter of fact, he prefers using pencils whenever possible, and he doesn't like to commit himself to anything in writing, and hence avoids writing letters. He feels he is easily distracted and, like many of these men, has a difficult time making decisions concerning major purchases such as cars, houses, and equipment. He will go back and forth on a purchasing decision for weeks and finally get so annoyed at himself that he goes out and buys anything, often the wrong thing.

He also hesitates at committing himself to a location and says he has lived in close to forty different apartments or houses during his adult life.

"A part of my lifestyle was always not knowing what I would be doing or where I would be the next day. I have to feel loose."

Philip does interesting work. His specialty is wildlife, and he travels extensively on assignment. He is never certain what part of the world he will be in from one moment to the next, and he takes many assignments in Africa and Asia. Although his schedule is loose and flexible, his work is the area where he is absolutely reliable. He prides himself on never missing a deadline, and his job has so many variables that he doesn't feel pinned down or trapped by it.

However, this is not the case in his personal life. As he quickly told me, for reasons he cannot explain he is reluctant to make plans and cannot be counted on to be reliable when his family and friends are involved.

"I have a reputation for not showing up. Whenever I promise to do something with someone, it makes me anxious. For
example, I recently made a commitment to go with my uncle
to a family birthday party. I like this uncle, and I want to
follow through on this commitment, but it is very very difficult
for me. Everyone who knows me well knows this about me.
I'm trying to train myself to think of these events in the same
way I think about business meetings, but it's not the same . . .
the relationships are different."

Philip's modus operandi with women has changed in the past
few years. When he was younger, he would meet a woman and
initiate the traditional pursuit. Many women I have spoken to
have met and been pursued by someone like Philip. When it
happens, they are very flattered. If the man seems sincere,
honest, and sensitive, they tend to believe his pursuit. It's easy
to believe and get involved with someone like Philip. It's also
easy to feel totally betrayed and disillusioned when he goes into
reverse. As Philip tells it:

"Until recently when I met someone I liked I would go
overboard in a sort of carefree, almost careless involvement
—to me at least. I would pay a lot of attention to her . . .
make many phone calls . . . buy flowers . . . send presents . . . see her for several nights in a row. This would last
about a week, and then reality would set in, and I would begin
an honest manipulation so we wouldn't get too close. Then I
would withdraw and be inaccessible and unavailable. Some
women have gotten very angry with me. One woman went
so far as to throw a brick through my window."

If a woman had been looking closely, she might have seen
the signs of commitmentphobia even when he was most actively
pursuing her. Among other things, he tends to compartmentalize
his life; the women he dates rarely get to meet his friends or
business associates. He has very specific phone behavior, which
is usually obvious even at the beginning of a relationship.

"It's interesting, but even when I felt like pursuing a woman,
I resisted giving out my home phone number. I never had
an answering machine, and it was always difficult reaching

me. I have a studio that I use, but they know me there, and I can make sure I don't get disturbed by unwanted calls.

"These days I tend not to ask for phone numbers either. Instead I'll suggest that the woman meet me at a specific spot such as a coffee shop, or a bar—often the spot where we first met—at the same time the following week. Then I'll decide whether or not I'll be there."

Philip says that he used to be amazingly promiscuous, but that he has changed. He realizes, however, that even though he has given up some of his more extreme behavior, he is probably still not acting like a man who wants to marry in the near future.

"Nowadays I try not to sleep with somebody unless I really think that there is a chance at a real relationship. However, when I tell you that I want a partner with a future, I also have to admit that the woman I'm seeing now is probably wrong for me. The tables are turned here. She doesn't want to get too close, and I'm the one asking for more time, more attention. But if she gave it to me, I don't think I would want to spend the rest of my life with her. There are too many problems, and I have too many reservations about her personally."

Philip says that he feels that his life is happier and more fulfilling than many, but he is disappointed in himself and in his inability to form a lasting love relationship.

"I did a horrible thing a year ago. I met a woman, dated her a few times, and fell in love with her. Then I met her children, a boy and a girl, and I fell in love with them. It was an instant family. I took them to zoos and parks and lakes. The kids were crazy about me . . . they even sent me Father's Day cards. And I was crazy about them. I thought, 'I want this family, this commitment.' So of course I proposed. I was on the greatest high. I was happier than I had ever been in my life. I felt really content and excited about the challenge of taking care of a family. I thought they would give me the motivation to settle down, work harder, make more money. When I met her, everything in my life felt very temporary—I didn't have a house, I didn't have a car.

In one fell swoop, the woman and I went shopping, and I took care of everything—my accountant thought I was going crazy. I had had no commitments until then, so I went out in a knee-jerk reaction to life and did it all. I went overboard. It was like being intoxicated."

Within days of Philip's euphoric proposing/purchasing binge, his alarm went off. From that moment on, all he could think about was getting out. At that point, there was nothing Philip's fiancé could have done to stop him. He didn't want to talk about it; he didn't want to work on the relationship; he didn't want to waste any time doing anything but making his exit.

"Then, just as suddenly, I sobered up. I saw all the things that were wrong with the woman. I didn't feel I could depend on her. Oh, I could depend on her loyalty and her love, but I couldn't go to her with a problem; I couldn't depend on her judgment. When she had a problem she went to an astrologer. I was depressed because I realized I didn't have the right to expect her to be different. She was working as a temporary receptionist; she had never had to take care of herself. I'm embarrassed by how stupid I was. I had to admit to friends that I had made this stupid mistake. I tried to make a clean break. I tried to tell her how I felt, but she wouldn't hear it. She didn't believe me, how could she? Only a few weeks before I had been acting as though I wanted to be everything to her and her children. It got really awful. She kept trying to get in touch with me. She asked me how I could have asked her to turn her life around without thinking it out. She was angry as well as determined to not let me get away. She made phone calls and sent letters, pleading, begging. She just couldn't accept my explanation. I decided not to give her any feedback at all and didn't take her phone calls or answer her letters. Finally it ended."

Philip's story about his aborted marriage plans is a quintessential example of commitmentphobia at its worst. But, interestingly enough, if you had heard this story from the woman's point of view, your first reaction would have been to wonder what *she* did wrong. Hearing it from Philip's side, it is amazingly clear that she did nothing wrong. The whole setup was Philip's doing. As Philip would be the first to tell, she hadn't even pressured him into proposing.

"After that relationship, I've been really gun-shy. I felt as though I had been blindfolded and put in front of a firing squad and then survived. I think the experience pushed me even further away from commitment in some ways. I haven't been very good at it when I tried it. When I asked this woman to marry me, there was nothing pressuring me to do it. Nobody told me to do it. She was surprised when it happened. Thrilled, but surprised. It was totally my doing, and I had nobody to blame but myself."

One might assume that Philip's willingness to take the blame for this relationship indicates that this was a learning experience for him. Yet further conversation revealed that this was not the first time he had retreated from the precipice of commitment.

"About ten years ago I proposed to a woman I had been living with. She was really adorable, and she would tease me about commitment, saying that I could never learn to use the "M" word. Well, I finally used the "M" word one night in a very passionate moment. But as I was proposing, it felt as though I were being caught in a lie. It felt like a parody, and was very strange. We set a date, had the invitations printed. We were engaged . . . I was so proud of myself for coming around and making a commitment. Then I was offered an assignment that would have conflicted with our marriage plans. I took the assignment and canceled the wedding. Somehow we never set another date—once I had asked her to marry me, I began to notice things about her. They had all been there before, but they hadn't mattered to me. Finally, one night I returned from working late, and she did something that really angered me, though truthfully, it was nothing very different than anything she had done before. She hadn't changed, but my perception of her had changed. I had suddenly had it. So I walked out. That was it."

In retrospect, Philip says that there were two other women in his life, when he was younger, with whom he might have been happy, but he left both of them because he didn't want to make a commitment.

"It's frightening how easy it is for me to walk away from something. I can walk away from my feelings overnight, and I've done it many times. It always takes a woman totally off guard."

Imagine a dimly lit restaurant bar near the ski slopes. There's a fire in the fireplace, and the pianist in the bar is playing Gershwin. It's off season so the bar is still quiet. That's where Philip was sitting the other night when he met an attractive, intelligent, responsible woman. It would seem that she had all the qualities he says he is looking for.

"We talked for hours, about everything—life, love, relationships. She was from out of town, and was staying with friends. She hesitated at giving me her phone number and asked me, instead, to give her mine. I didn't do it. I just didn't want to give her my phone number. She said that she would be at a specific restaurant the following night with friends and I could meet her there again if I wanted to. I didn't do it. The fantasy was just fine. I didn't want it to go any further."

Philip feels he is changing and thinks that the fact that he recently bought both a house and a car was a major step.

"It was hard—buying a car. There's a lot of cars out there, and it was hard to make a choice as to which kind to buy, but I'm determined not to second-guess my choice and look over my shoulder at every other car and wonder if I made the right choice. For the first time, I put a home address on my driver's license. I never did that before. The big event in my life will be when I put my name on the mailbox. To me that will be a commitment to stay in one place."

It's easy to see why a woman who meets Philip would be attracted to what he says about his desire to form a permanent attachment or commitment to one person. Yet, despite his sincerity, it's equally easy to see that something has kept him from committing himself to any person, place, or thing for even a brief period of time, and that it would be foolhardy for any woman to think that it would be different with her.

GARY: *A thirty-two-year-old sales rep for a major book company—single.*

When I met Gary for the first time, he was about to go on his third date with Janet, a woman he had met the week before. Gary met Janet on a blind date. Since he got out of college, Gary figures he has gone on approximately six hundred blind dates, and this is the way he meets most of the women he goes out with.

Gary's blind date statistics are more than amusing; they are a clear indication that he is always maintaining distance. By using blind dates as a vehicle for meeting women, rather than everyday social or work situations, Gary has made sure that he will not have to see these women again if he doesn't want to—and sooner or later, Gary doesn't want to.

Because Gary said he was very busy, I met him at his apartment and accompanied him in his car while he drove to pick up his date. Gary said he had been living in his apartment for two years. The only pieces of furniture were two couches still wrapped in plastic. He said he had bought them a few months before but was thinking of returning them and hence had never taken them out of their covers.

Janet, Gary's date, was turning twenty-eight that day, and Gary had planned a "special" birthday evening. He was taking her to a very expensive restaurant for dinner. Afterward, he had tickets to a hit musical at a theater near where he lives. He had done some business with one of the owners of the theater and while I was waiting to interview him, Gary was on the phone trying to make arrangements for the entire cast to come out and sing "Happy Birthday" to Janet. Gary said he thought she would be thrilled by this. When I heard all of this planning going on, I commented that Janet must be pretty special to Gary. He looked at me as though I was extremely dense, and told me that he barely knew her.

Gary goes out almost every night and estimates that he has been out with fifty new women in the past year. He says he can tell a lot about a woman just from the initial phone contact.

"For example, beware of women who give great phone. It can be deceiving. There are women who are terrific on the phone the first time, and then when you meet them, it's like it's not the same girl. That's the reason I don't talk too much on the phone now before I meet them . . . I don't want to be disappointed."

Gary has been out with so many women, it is hard for him to keep them apart. He puts it best when he says, "Sometimes I think I need a flow chart."

Gary has never had a relationship that was truly monogamous. Although there have been brief periods when he was only sleeping with one woman, he is always dating, always searching.

Gary has never really told a woman that he loved her, but he did once propose to a woman he describes as the "love of my life." Sharon was a woman he met in college, and he continued to see her after graduation. All together they went out, off and on, for four or five years. But don't let that number fool you. During that period of time, they slept together no more than half a dozen times because Sharon was, as Gary now realizes, "difficult" and not that interested in him. She also had several really major problems: She was spoiled, and she had a drug problem that Gary assumed she would "outgrow." She never did. Gary, it goes without saying, has never been involved with drugs and had no idea of the ramifications of such a problem when he proposed.

Gary says he used to tell minor white lies to women, but now he tries very hard to always be honest and above board. He also tries to keep it friendly, and he has an admirable record of keeping the women he goes out with friendly toward him, although he says a few women who expected more from him have become angry.

Gary says that until recently he never spent an entire night in a woman's apartment or allowed one to stay with him.

"I didn't want them to think I might be serious, so I would make a point of leaving after sex, even if it was two or three in the morning. It was like going to a ball game. I got very tired sometimes. Now, I try to make it clear in other ways.

Some girls have tried to make me feel guilty for not responding the way they want me to, but I don't feel responsible."

Last year, Gary got seriously involved with someone. He says he didn't expect it to happen because she lived in a different state. Since she was Gary's first serious relationship in almost ten years, one must speculate that the only reason it *did* happen was that she lived in a different state and the distance was insured, a given. But even two hours of plane travel each way was not enough to keep the relationship from reaching the "sticky" point.

"At the end we were commuting back and forth almost every weekend. One night we were at my parents' country house—they were away—and after making love I couldn't fall asleep. Allison had been talking about marriage—she was a couple of years older than me and was worried about having children. Well, first I couldn't sleep, and then I had an anxiety attack. My heart started palpitating and I began sweating. I didn't know it was an anxiety attack at the time. Well, a week passed, and it didn't really get better. My heart was racing all the time. Then I began losing weight. I got scared, so finally I went to my doctor.

"He ran a whole series of tests and could find nothing wrong. Then he remembered something I had forgotten: The same thing had happened in college when I got into a serious relationship with a girl.

"I was certainly infatuated with Allison. She was terrific. But when my stomach went bad, and I couldn't eat anymore, that's when I knew I had to end the relationship. I did, and I immediately felt better."

Gary recently took a trip to California for a week. Before arriving, he called some business friends and told them he would love to meet some new women. He arrived on Sunday. Monday he spent the day with Liza. She took the day off from work, and they spent it at Disneyland. Gary said she was a "really nice woman" with whom he had a "great day." He felt she had a lot to offer, but he could see that "nothing was going to happen."

On Tuesday evening, he had a date with another woman, Sally, who he really found attractive. He took her to a good restaurant for dinner, and then to a show. They took a bottle of wine and went back to her apartment, but right after they started necking she mentioned some crazed killer who was breaking into women's apartments, and killing the boyfriends. It turned him off, and he went home—but he wanted to see her again, "preferably not in Southern California." On Wednesday he had a date with Renee so he couldn't see Sally from the night before. He did call her but he didn't want to tell her that he had another blind date. She said that she was going to be East in a few months and maybe she could see him then. Renee, the third blind date, was "cute," but he didn't like her as much as Sally. He might have seen both of them again, but the next day he decided to drive to San Diego. There he picked up a fourth woman, Gwen, who he spent the day with.

When he got back to his hotel, he found a card from Sally saying that she really hoped they would get together again. He phoned her before he left to confirm that he would be back in California soon and might see her then, if not during the holidays in Boston. He also phoned Renee, as well as Gwen, the woman from San Diego, and told them both that he might be back in L.A. He did not phone the first woman, Liza, even though he had a terrific time at Disneyland because he said he could see she wanted "something serious" in her life.

Gary has a five date policy. It goes something like this:

DATE ONE: A drink, or lunch, or brunch. Something short and sweet.

DATE TWO: Dinner, and then some heavy necking.

DATE THREE: Dinner, possibly a movie or a show. Then back to the apartment for more necking.

DATE FOUR: A movie and back to the apartment with a bottle of wine, and you sleep together.

DATE FIVE: Daytime date. A museum, the zoo, etc. You size up the situation and you decide whether you are going to ask her out again.

You might think it strange that Gary needs to have five dates before he knows whether or not to continue. This is how he explained it.

"You need to see somebody a few times if you want to sleep with her. But then you need to sleep with her to know whether you want to do it again. Often it's not chemistry propelling you into bed; it's just the challenge. More often than not, once I've slept with a woman, I don't want to do it again. But how would I know this if I didn't sleep with her? And how am I going to sleep with her if I don't go out with her a few times? Hence the five date system."

Gary is always very difficult to pin down, which is why I wound up interviewing him in his car on his way to a date. As you can imagine from his social life, he doesn't have much extra time. Although he insists that he ultimately wants marriage and all the trimmings, he said he sees little chance of it happening in the near future.

"When I look at my married friends, with the babies and houses and meetings and station wagons, I don't understand it. They get involved with other couples and they get boring. That's what it all seems to me. Boring."

I phoned Gary a month or so after our automobile interview to clear up a few questions, and I asked him what had happened to Janet, the date he was going on the day we met—the one for whom he wanted to have an entire cast sing "Happy Birthday."

At first he couldn't remember what I was talking about. Then, when he did, he told me he never asked her out again.

"I decided I didn't like her that much. It was a terrific date though . . . she was really thrilled. One of my friends is in the florist business so I brought her a dozen roses. She loved that, too."

Gary tells most of the women he dates that all he wants to do is find Ms. Right and settle down and have a family. Given his track record, it's hard to take him seriously. In truth, it would appear that Gary spends too little time with any one woman to do much serious damage. I get the impression that women look back on their experiences with Gary more puzzled than pained.

MARK: A thirty-one-year-old art teacher—single.

Mark is probably dangerous to women because he looks so safe. If you accept what he first tells you, he appears to be a very lonely guy who desperately wants love and marriage. His apparent vulnerability tends to make a woman go out of her way to make him feel more secure. This is a mistake, because once Mark perceives that the woman might expect commitment, he responds by going out of his way to sabotage the relationship and in the process usually manages to make the *woman* feel completely insecure.

When I first started thinking about this book, I couldn't stop talking about my initial research. I was doing just that one night at a large party, when a woman approached me and suggested that I meet her friend Mark. The woman, who had known Mark for many years, said that he prefaced every conversation by expressing his feelings of loneliness and need for a permanent commitment, but she explained that all of his friends were beginning to feel that Mark might be less than sincere in what he articulated. It seems that he had made it very clear to those who knew him that he would never settle down with any woman who wasn't Jewish. However, as far as anyone knew, he had also never gone out with a woman who *was* Jewish.

Mark, who is thirty-five, has always lived in cities with large Jewish populations. It was difficult for this woman to believe that it was totally accidental that he had never dated a Jewish woman. The friend stressed that Mark was quite brilliant. She said that at the Ivy League college they had both attended he was considered extremely talented, and everyone expected him to go on to make a major splash in the art world.

I was about to go out on a book tour, and when I phoned Mark, he agreed to meet me at his apartment in the suburbs of the large midwestern city where he was working as an art teacher. Mark, a tall, wiry-looking man, with a darting energetic body that moves almost as quickly as his brain, met me at the door of his spacious one-bedroom apartment. Although the apartment was pleasantly large and bright, it had a decidedly unfinished look, and Mark said he was unsure of how long he was going to be there. He gestured around the apartment after I arrived, and said, "It needs a woman's touch, huh?"

I was immediately struck by the dozens of photographs on the walls. Everywhere I looked I saw two young children, who Mark said were his nieces. In several of the pictures, Mark was there, also, helping them toss fish to the seals at the zoo, bringing in the birthday cake. In these shots, he was all smiles, very much the doting uncle. If a woman were to come into his apartment, the photographs would tend to reinforce Mark's version of his life—all he wants is Mrs. Right and Baby Right. The only other photographs in the apartment were of Mark and some college friends, and one, very prominently displayed on his desk, of a woman who I learned was Mark's last girlfriend, Jane.

I had a good time interviewing Mark because he was consistently funny and perceptive. Like his friends, he was painfully aware of the inconsistencies between some of what he said and what he did. For a man who says he wants marriage, he has a couple of very effective techniques for warding off commitment: Mark never dates women who pass his criteria for commitment, and Mark never lets a relationship grow past a certain point.

The week that I interviewed him, Mark was briefly taking care of a couple of cats for a neighbor who was away. He said his reactions were indicative of his conflict; he was torn because he resented being tied to a regular schedule, but he was so lonely and isolated that he was grateful to the cats for their temporary companionship. He said he would not be able to deal with the commitment required by a pet of his own and barely managed to keep a few plants, which he "maintained in a state of pure terror."

We started out talking about work. Although Mark was good at his job and had received recognition for it, he was quick to point out that he wasn't really an art teacher—this was just something he was doing until he could sort out his life.

"Mentally, I'm just not into my job. It's not at all challenging—but I find it hard to focus or commit myself in any major way to anything, including my own work. It's all short-lived . . . I'm going from one thing to another, and I keep hoping I will find the one thing that will tie it all together, be it career or spouse."

He readily acknowledged that his anxieties about commitment reached into all areas of his life.

"My commitment anxieties are the focal point of my life. I think about it constantly . . . but it's not just women, it's everything. For example, three years ago, I decided I wanted a computer. As always, I shopped myself into exhaustion, and I still couldn't make up my mind. Would a newer one be coming out with better features? Would a less expensive one be coming out? Would one of the ones already on the market cost less the following year? I couldn't make a decision, so I decided to temporarily rent a computer. Three years later, even I had to draw the line. I had spent three times the price of any computer in order to rent a product which was inferior to the one I wanted. So I jumped in and bought an inexpensive model. It's okay, but it's typical that it is missing several features I need, so now I've started comparison shopping all over again."

Loneliness is a recurrent theme in Mark's conversation—he said he couldn't imagine living the rest of his life without a permanent commitment. Mark said that he had had very few relationships with women and those had been short-lived. He had no recollection of any one night stands or casual sexual encounters. He also felt that he didn't have a history of leaving women without an explanation, but, when pressed, he remembered that it had happened once. He had been seeing a woman for a short period of time, and, in bed one night, he decided that he didn't want to be there. He said he got up without an explanation, put on his clothes, said he was going out for a few minutes, and never returned or spoke to her again. He saw her in a movie theater a year later and went out of his way to avoid her.

By his own admission, Mark often forgets not only the details surrounding his relationships with women, but also what he was feeling at the time. Only two women seemed to emerge as ones with whom he shared strong emotions.

His relationship with Andrea lasted only two months, but his friends remembered him being quite enthralled with her. From what he had told them about the affair, they were under the impression that she had rejected him. As I discovered, this was not the case.

Mark admitted that he was unusually attracted to Andrea. It was, according to him, a very tempestuous and passionate two months. He also liked her a great deal.

"We had a lot in common emotionally and intellectually, but she had two major flaws. She smoked, and she wasn't Jewish. At the beginning, for a couple of weeks or so, I fantasized about marriage, but when I told her that I loved her, I realized I wasn't totally comfortable doing so. On a basic level I knew I wouldn't be able to marry her. I remember one night when the sex was particularly loving, and I guess I got carried away in terms of what I said. Afterward I felt as though I should have issued a disclaimer."

Mark readily admits that he doesn't like to be the one to end a relationship. Instead, as he did with Andrea, he indulges in such provocative behavior that the woman confronts him.

"When I realized that I couldn't avoid the fact that she would ultimately want marriage, I soured the relationship by becoming sullen and moody. She ended the relationship, but I pushed her into it. We went to a party one night, and I was withdrawn and avoiding her. She finally confronted me. She told me she loved me, but she didn't think the relationship had a future. Although I would certainly have wanted to go on seeing her, I couldn't argue with the accuracy of her perceptions. I was pretty upset and depressed when this one ended, but she was right—I wasn't going to marry her, no matter what she did."

It's interesting to note that although Mark claims that it is hard for him to meet and attract women, he is amazingly quick to end relationships, even when they are satisfying.

Unlike most of the men I interviewed, Mark does not appear to be overwhelmingly aggressive in pursuing a new woman. Most of his relationships grow out of work or social situations where he has more time to sell himself. As we talked, it became apparent to him as well as to me that his pursuit was very strong, albeit very subtle.

When Mark is interested in a woman, he immediately involves her in intimate discussions of his life, his anxieties, his problems, etc. He realizes that he goes fairly overboard in portraying himself as a man who is searching for a woman who will make a difference in his life, and that a woman might construe his apparent vulnerability with her as a sign that she is "the one" who will alter his history.

This dynamic was very apparent in a recent relationship. It was perhaps the longest and most meaningful one in Mark's life. He worked with Jane and had known her almost a year before they began going out together. He was very attracted to her and did everything he could to interest her. By the time they slept together, she knew all there was to know about him and surprised him by being totally accepting of all his quirks. Although he felt more comfortable and secure with her than he had in any previous relationship, it ultimately ended because he knew he could not marry a non-Jewish woman.

As he had with Andrea, Mark told Jane that he loved her, but he said that he felt less guilty about it because he realized that love meant different things to different people. He felt that if Jane wanted to know if love to him meant, "I will live with you for ever and ever," she should have asked.

Since Jane knew Mark's views on interfaith marriages, I asked him how she could have continued, and he acknowledged that he might have led her astray.

"Someplace at the beginning, before we slept together, I think I told her that if I felt strongly enough about a woman, I would probably overlook the Jewish issue. I think she wanted to believe that I ultimately would do just that. She was definitely very committed to me. After we slept together she asked a lot of questions about Judaism, and I projected down the road that if I was committed I would ask her to convert. I may have said something vague like if I wanted to marry a non-Jewish woman, I might ask the woman to convert, and since she had no strong feelings on the issue, she may have considered this a possibility—she didn't ask really straight

questions, and I didn't want to rock the boat. I never told her
that it would be impossible, because I imagined that if I did
the relationship would have ended, and I didn't want that to
happen, at least not in the beginning."

But within a couple of months after they started sleeping
together, Mark began drawing away emotionally. He had a dozen
reasons for doing this, reasons why he thought Jane was un-
suitable for him.

"I had other reservations about Jane. She never had the
breaks I did, and she had to work when she went to school.
She knew I felt that she wasn't as well educated as I might
have liked, and so she applied to graduate school. She changed
politically and started paying more attention to the world
around her. She started reading the newspaper cover to cover,
and she bought books and magazines and went to museums
to learn more about art. She even stopped smoking."

It is fairly apparent from all of this that Jane was sincerely
interested in Mark. It appears that she believed him when he
found fault with specifics about her, and she went out of her
way to change. But, as is often the case, her goodwill and good
intentions did not influence Mark's behavior. Nor did it make
him tell her straight out that it wasn't going to work.

"I think all the ways she changed ultimately helped her,
so I don't feel guilty about any of this. But there's no question
that she had high hopes of becoming for me the kind of woman
I would want, and I suppose I gave her no reason to believe
that this wasn't possible. Most of my messages were fairly
obscure. When she started talking about long-range plans, for
example, like vacations and holidays, I sort of stalled. This is
a pattern of mine—I tend to put women off instead of giving
a definite no."

Although at the beginning Mark and Jane were seeing each
other four or five times a week, they continued to maintain their
distance at work. Mark felt it was important that none of their
co-workers suspect that they had anything other than a business
relationship. One of these co-workers, a woman named Debbie,

had a role to play in the breakup. For whatever it's worth, she was also not Jewish.

"I knew and was friendly with Debbie before I became involved with Jane, but it wasn't until Jane and I became intimate that I looked at Debbie as anything more than a friend. Jane gave me a great deal. There's no question that I felt more confident about myself as a man because of my relationship with Jane, and that may have played a part in this . . . also, undeniably, I could have been using Debbie as a means of distancing myself from Jane. I don't know . . . I ultimately never slept with Debbie, but my relationship with her, and my fantasies about her, were certainly a part of the breakup."

I have to stop and comment here once again on what should be fairly obvious. Before he began dating Jane, Mark had no girlfriend; there had been no women in his life to speak of. He had been desperately lonely and was feeling very insecure with women in general. When Jane entered his life, by his admission, for the first time he had a fully gratifying sexual relationship with a woman who had been his friend for a full year before they began sleeping together. One would imagine that he might be able to enjoy the relationship, even temporarily. Some people might even suggest that he should just shut up and be grateful. Instead, within months, he began to act in such a way that his relationship with Jane was doomed.

Mark had told Jane about his friendship with Debbie, explaining to her, and he truly believed it at the time, that he could not tell Debbie about his relationship with Jane. Jane had reacted by being hurt and jealous. If his relationship with Debbie was just a friendship, as Mark kept telling her, why, she asked, should she be excluded? And if it was such a close friendship, why didn't Mark want to tell her about the woman in his life?

"What finally happened is that I decided to take a trip at a time Jane couldn't get off from work. Debbie, on the other hand, could, and really wanted to come along—so we set out in a car for Canada.

"Nothing happened between us, but I knew that I hadn't

missed Jane as much as I should have. When I returned, Jane was waiting in the apartment, eager to see me; she looked really pretty and she had ordered in a special meal for the two of us. I, on the other hand, was tired and grubby—I sort of avoided any physical contact with her and went to bed, and sleep, as quickly as possible. I guess I became more and more moody and grumpy with her after that. From that point on, it got really bad."

"Jane was still accommodating and catering to me, and I, of course, had very mixed feelings about it. I liked it, but I knew she didn't realize that as far as I was concerned the relationship was over, so I felt guilty and uncomfortable around her. She was still working on the relationship, and I was trying to subtly communicate that it wouldn't last. The guiltier I felt, the testier and moodier I became. The nicer she got, the more annoyed I became, because I wanted to turn the relationship around and get out of it. I would tell myself that she was only being nice because she was trying to get what she wanted."

At the beginning of the relationship, when Jane had been nice to Mark, he saw her behavior as a sign of her superior character and judgment; she had chosen him for her favors. Once he wanted to leave the relationship, however, he began to find other explanations for her basic goodwill, and he decided that she was trying to manipulate him. So many men have said something similar to me. If a woman is pained by rejective behavior, for example, some men deny the honesty of the woman's feelings and decide she is trying to manipulate the man with her feelings. Unlike many men, Mark was ultimately honest enough to realize that Jane was just being Jane, a warm, giving woman.

"I would try to add distance between us by staging arguments over insignificant subjects whenever things between us got too easy and too comfortable. So we went on like that for a few weeks, with me trying to throw a wrench into the machine while she tried to make it work. She couldn't help being aware that I was being testy with her. I think it was my guilt over the fact that I knew I wasn't going to marry her that made me nasty. Also, we were seeing each other less and less in a social way. Finally, after a few weeks like this, Jane confronted me while we were on a hiking trip. It was fairly unpleasant . . . we had to go back with her crying all the way. I wouldn't have planned the end that way."

Mark has worked at staying friendly with Jane, who began looking for a new job soon after the relationship ended. She was fortunate enough to find one with a better title and a higher salary, and is undoubtedly more successful. Mark acknowledges that the relationship was the best one he had ever had.

"There is no question but that we communicated well. On one level it was a very honest, intimate relationship, but on another, because of what I didn't tell her, of course it was a very dishonest relationship."

Mark doesn't know why he hasn't met a Jewish woman, but he acknowledges that religion plays an important role in his ambivalent attitude toward women and marriage.

"The fact that the woman isn't Jewish is definitely a safety valve. In my mind, with a Jewish woman, there would be no escape. By definition it would be so messy it would be impossible."

Mark says that when he sleeps in the same bed with a woman, he often has difficulty breathing, and he wakes with a definite trapped feeling. The women he has slept with have all remarked on the breathing. Mark explained:

"I wake up with a trapped feeling, a definite trapped feeling, and I feel depressed. The women I've slept with all say that every time I breathe, it sounds like a heavy sigh. I'm really just breathing, but it sounds like I'm sighing. It went away with Jane; she's the only one I ever got over it with. But with Jane it was not a true trap because there was a built-in reason to get out of the relationship—religion. But that's why I don't go out with many Jewish women. It's fear—fear that there will be more pressure to make a commitment. But once I know a relationship is a dead end, it's very depressing, very artificial. "The women never think I'm snoring, they always describe it as a sigh. They think I'm sad. I am."

<u>BRAD</u>: *a forty-eight-year-old filmmaker, divorced.*

Although at first glance it may seem like a contradiction, some worst-case commitmentphobics are drawn to marriage. Most of these men don't like living alone and want to be able to share their lives with a woman. However, typically, no sooner has one of these men said, "I do," than his inner phobic voice begins screaming, "get me out of here!"

Such a man tends to believe it is his chosen mate rather than the situation that is causing his distress and may divorce and re-marry several times. Brad is an excellent example of a commit-mentphobic who marries and marries and marries and marries.

At forty-eight, Brad, a tall, good-looking filmmaker, is con-templating marriage for the fifth time. He would be the first to tell you that he is a questionable marriage candidate.

"It may seem odd to say this, considering my history, but I have always been genuinely reluctant to get married. As a matter of fact, I didn't want to get married any of the times that I did so and always regarded marriage as a trap. I probably could have saved a lot of people a lot of unhappiness if I followed these instincts. But I've also been in love with the women I've married. It would be fair to say that I pulled out all the stops when I was first interested in them. I drove miles to see them, wrote poetry, etc. Then the moment comes when it starts getting serious and I would think, 'How can I get out of this?' Then one day, it's too late, and you really can't get out without looking like a criminal."

Brad married twice while he was still in his early twenties. At that time, he was busy getting a law degree which he never used. Both marriages were brief. His third marriage, which lasted twelve years, was the longest, and he and this wife had four children.

"This third wife was the one to whom I was most commit-ted, in my own half-hearted way. She was very beautiful, and there were times that I was very much in love with her, but I was disgustingly unfaithful to her and started having affairs within a year of marriage. I would meet women and tell my wife I was working late. In the beginning, she wanted to believe me, so she believed me; she thought I was intensely hard-working. Eventually I became more flagrant, and she found out."

Brad says that he compounded the problem by blaming his wife.

"I felt intensely guilty about all my affairs and would justify my actions by telling myself that my wife was cold sexually. I would criticize the way she made love. This, of course, set up a vicious cycle. Understandably, she became less and less interested in making love.

"I also belittled those things she did well. I would go home, and she would be there peacefully reading to the children, dinner bubbling on the stove and instead of being happy, resentment would well up in me. I resented all her domesticity which symbolized the marital trap. So I would make fun of her. I blamed her for all my discomfort, did the old 'I'm misunderstood' routine, and found any number of phony rationalizations for my behavior."

Brad says that he is aware that his wife would have done anything she could to please him, but there was nothing she could do.

"My wife was very much in love with me, and I managed to ruin it. I'm still guilty over that. She just wanted to be a good wife—she was a lovely woman, a fabulous homemaker. She was devoted and hardworking; she baked, she ironed, she sewed. It would make any normal American male happy, but every home-cooked meal to me was like another nail in my coffin. I thought I just wanted to get out."

During this marriage, Brad got involved in a rather complicated and intense affair with a married woman who suggested that they divorce their respective mates and marry each other. Ironically, Brad says this woman's intensity made him regard his unhappy marriage as a safe and protected haven, and shortly after the divorce/re-marriage issue was raised, the affair ended.

Though he says that he thought he would be delighted to have the opportunity to leave his third marriage, when the break-up actually happened, Brad was devastated.

"Finally after twelve years, my behavior got to be too much for my wife and she became interested in another man. She told me she wanted a divorce. I literally fell into a deep depression. It was amazing, considering the circumstances. I asked her to please try again, but she would have none of it. At the time I was very bitter and blamed her for everything. Now, I realize that she acted in justifiable self-defense. I have the greatest respect for this woman who was much too good for me."

After his third marriage ended Brad, who also has a history of many career changes, moved to another city to work. There he met a woman with whom he had a five-year relationship. Although he was not totally faithful to this woman, whom he describes as being "perfect" for him, his affairs were limited.

When he and this woman had been together for two years, they made plans to share an apartment. She moved into the apartment they found together, but when the time came for Brad to do the same he balked. He says he neglected to answer his phone for several days before finally confronting the woman and telling her that he couldn't go through with the move. Although money was a problem, Brad was never able to give up his own space, even though he ended up spending practically every night with the woman in the joint apartment.

"After several years of this, *I* raised the issue of marriage —a definite mistake since she had never talked about it. After that, she became anxious to formalize our relationship and issued an ultimatum—marriage or else."

Brad chose "or else" and ended the relationship. It took him a very short time to start an affair with another woman. And this time he married again. The marriage was very brief and by his account "very stormy."

It was interesting interviewing Brad because he was eager to talk about his problems with commitment. He was genuinely appalled by his behavior with women and worried that he would never be able to change.

"A part of me thinks the reason I've had a lot of jobs and a lot of women is because I'm unique, imaginative, and adventurous. But another part of me knows I don't want to have only one job or one woman because I don't want to be identified with any one thing.

"I've used all sorts of excuses to get away from women. I remember once being with a woman I was deeply in love with and I would say to her, 'We're going to get married . . . we've got to be together.' And the woman would answer, 'We have too many problems . . . there are too many things to overcome.' And I would tell her, 'love will overcome everything.'

"Finally, she began to believe what I was saying, and one day she looked at me and said, 'Maybe you're right.' Immediately I began to feel worried. 'My god,' I thought, 'you idiot . . . Why didn't you leave it alone—the way it was before? Why did you have to go and spoil everything?' "

Brad is another example of a commitmentphobic who is a committed and involved father.

"I learned how to commit myself to my children. I suppose one could avoid that commitment as well, but I haven't done so. Perhaps it's because society looks more unfavorably upon a man who treats his children poorly than a man who treats his wife poorly. There is no question that the shame of being an unfeeling parent would be much worse than the shame of being an unfeeling husband. Whatever the reason, I'm responsible to my children."

Part 2
YOUR
RELATIONSHIP

What A Smart Woman Can Do

Chapter 7

UNDERSTANDING THE COMMITMENTPHOBIC RELATIONSHIP

WHAT A SMART WOMAN CAN DO

Now you know why some men can't love. So what can you do about it—or is there anything you can do? Yes, there is something you can do, and that's what this book is all about. Granted, *some* men are so commitmentphobic that their girlfriends could move across the Atlantic, and they would still feel trapped. Most of these men will never be able to love, and the smartest, most self-protective thing a woman can do is identify the problem and get out—before he does. By the time you finish reading this section, you should have the insight needed to recognize these worst-case commitmentphobics.

But not all commitmentphobics are *that* troubled. The vast majority of them *are* capable of loving and *are* capable of committing. But take notice: A relationship can take many paths—both good and bad—depending upon how a woman handles herself and how she relates to the man.

If you are involved with such a man, you probably sense that he wants to be able to love. However, another part of him—the commitmentphobic part—wants to run away. With this kind of internal conflict going on, this man is not going to be much help. Therefore, if you don't want to become another commitmentphobic statistic, it's up to you to clearly establish the ground rules that will provide a foundation for success.

Up until this point, this book has primarily dwelled on what the commitmentphobic does in a relationship. Now it's time to talk about you, the woman who attracted him in the first place.

IDENTIFYING THE WOMAN WHO GETS INVOLVED WITH A COMMITMENTPHOBIC

If you are currently involved or have ever been involved with a commitmentphobic, chances are that you have certain characteristics that this man finds appealing. Often these characteristics represent qualities that he lacks. These differences in character and personality help explain how the commitmentphobic's relationship gets off the ground, as well as why it often ends so badly.

In the beginning, when you first meet, the commitmentphobic typically goes into high gear. It's all hyper, a no-holds-barred come-on. He wants you. So he phones, writes, goes out of his way to be with you, and generally does whatever is necessary to get you to respond.

This man, at the beginning, appears to be utterly romantic. In reality, he is often totally unrealistic. He has no idea what it is he really wants, and he has no concept of how his behavior might be interpreted.

He is probably somebody with little history of reliability and dependability in other relationships. Most of this behavior was caused by his commitmentphobia, but because he becomes uncomfortable whenever he thinks about commitment, he prefers *not* to think about it—at least not realistically.

You, on the other hand, probably have a history of total reliability and dependability. You pride yourself on the fact that people can count on you. In essence, you do what you say you're going to do. Consequently, you think long and hard before you say you will do anything. If you came on to anyone the way he comes on to you, it would mean something. It would mean that you were prepared to do everything possible to try and develop a real, long-term relationship.

Therefore at the very beginning, because you live up to what you promise, you don't promise much. When you first meet, you don't move as quickly; you have to be somewhat convinced that his feelings and intentions are sincere before you respond in kind. This need to be convinced is self-protective and sensible. The problem is that you use the wrong criteria to judge what he says he feels about you. You interpret his behavior in the same way that you would interpret yours. You assume he thinks the way you think. You assume that he has the same goals that you do. You assume that he has the same level of emotional integrity that you have. But how can he? He is a totally conflicted man: It's not that he doesn't want you—it's just that he can't handle what you want. It's not that he doesn't want love, it's just that when he thinks about the real commitment that love brings, he is overwhelmed by anxiety.

If you are involved with a commitmentphobic, you have to understand that everything he does elicits typical responses from women. These responses are part love and part programming. By definition, these responses tend to (a) reinforce a commitment-phobic's problem and (b) lead to the destructive entity I refer to as "The Commitmentphobic Relationship."

IDENTIFYING THE COMMITMENTPHOBIC RELATIONSHIP

In this section, I've broken the typical commitmentphobic relationship down into stages. Each stage has a definite dynamic of its own—a dynamic which is acted out through a variety of readily identifiable steps. As you read, you will see that each step is outlined as follows: First, there is a description of what the man does. Second, there is a description of the way a woman typically responds. Third, there is a discussion of what a commitment-phobic is thinking and feeling. Fourth, and finally, there is a discussion of how a smart woman *should* respond, and what she can do to keep the relationship from plummeting into commitment-phobic oblivion.

Please keep in mind, as you read this, that not all men act out every single one of these steps. Also, in some short, intense relationships, the commitmentphobic may panic prematurely. When this happens, much of the Middle and End may be skipped, and the man heads straight for the Bitter End. In these cases, much of the conflict is played out in the commitmentphobic's head. But for the vast majority of these relationships, these are the classic steps.

HOW TO USE THIS SECTION

This section is designed to help you:

1. Identify the commitmentphobic before you get involved —not after.

2. Recognize how, in the beginning of these relationships, women typically fail to protect themselves, setting the stage for tremendous emotional damage later on.

3. Acknowledge how certain behavior patterns—such as setting boundaries, fault-finding, mixed messages—are almost universal indications of a commitmentphobic problem in general, and are not specifically directed against you.

4. Learn why typical reactions such as "showering him with love" or "appealing to his better tendencies" only aggravate his problem.

5. Recognize the sign language that he uses to tell a woman that he wants to get out.

6. Learn to recognize and understand the true meaning— both positive and negative—behind his commitmentphobic patter.

7. Learn how to recognize a "no win" situation for what it is, and how to extricate yourself from the relationship with as little personal damage as possible.

8. Recognize a worst-case commitmentphobic for what he is—not for what you wish he could become.

9. Learn how, from the very beginning, you can structure a relationship to minimize his commitmentphobic tendencies and maximize your chances for healthy, positive relationship growth.

Chapter 8

THE BEGINNING OF A COMMITMENTPHOBIC RELATIONSHIP

THE BEGINNING

No question about it: In the Beginning, the commitment-phobic is totally ardent and romantic. What a woman has to remember is that he is also totally unrealistic and has no practical sense of what he is saying or doing. All he can think about is getting you involved as quickly as possible. Because he isn't thinking long-term, he has no reason to hold anything back. Whatever romantic words come into his mind, he says. Whatever gift strikes his fancy, he buys. Whatever he can do or say to make you want him and love him, he does. It's as simple as that. He is so fixated on you at this point that it is hard to believe that he could ever change. But if he is a true commitmentphobic, and if the relationship moves too quickly, he will probably panic.

What a woman must do at the Beginning is stay realistic and slow the relationship down. At the Beginning, you have a great deal of ego leverage and control. Use it to set the pace and tone that will lead to permanency. No matter how much you're tempted to go along with his "Hollywood" style, don't do it. And remember:

■ The Beginning can last an hour, a week, a month or a year; it all depends on how long it takes you to respond.

■ If he sweeps you off your feet too quickly, he will become terrified of the level of commitment expected of him.

■ You have to set the pace, and slow and steady is definitely the way to go.

The Typical Pattern

1. He comes on strong and is probably more interested in you than you are in him.

Your Typical Response:

When you first meet him, you may not be interested in him. As a matter of fact, you may even be distinctly uninterested. The majority of the women we spoke to reported that they initially thought the man was too "different" in terms of interests and lifestyle. A typical woman's reaction: "I couldn't figure out what made him so attracted to me. At first, I thought he was making a mistake. But he sure did make me feel desirable."

His Agenda:

The commitmentphobic pulls out all the stops in his pursuit because he is thinking about today, not tomorrow. Totally *now*-oriented, he's trying to make everything special and wonderful and romantic *today*. For the moment, he's not concerned about the long-range consequences of what he says or does. He just wants you to respond. One of the most obvious ways to get you to respond is through sex. A man knows that when a woman agrees to go to bed with him, it usually indicates a greater acceptance on her part. He wants that acceptance.

The Smart Response:

The stronger he comes on, the more skeptical you should be.

When a man is immediately overwhelmed by you, warning signals should go off in your brain. Here's what they should say: This man responds more to fantasy than he does to reality.

Unless you exercise caution, this quality will come back to haunt the relationship, and you, later. (It's easy to be flattered, but keep in mind that for all he knows about you, you could be an alien life form.) Instead of being flattered, pay close attention to *him*. Notice everything he says and does, as well as everything he *doesn't* say and *doesn't* do.

Listen to your instincts and not his sales pitch, and don't allow yourself to be swept off your feet, joining him in fantasy land. Also:

■ Don't rush into bed because he seems to want it so badly.

■ Don't assume his desire to rush you into bed means that he is in the throes of a greater passion than any other man has known.

■ Don't rush into bed because you are guilty about the money, time, or energy he has spent.

■ And, most important, don't rush into bed because you think once the focus is off sex, the relationship will stabilize.

Even though he is pushing for closeness, maintain your distance. Come to an evaluation of his character and emotional makeup based upon your own best instincts—not based upon what he tells you about himself. The more he is pushing, the more you should be slowing him down. If he gets impatient and leaves, he would have done the same thing later, causing you far greater heartache.

A possibility to consider: At the beginning, is he so intensely interested in you because you are not that interested in him?

2. Within a very short time, he indicates that he thinks you are "special" and seems to have few if any reservations about you or his decision to pursue you.

Your Typical Response:

He makes you feel totally accepted, and it's a wonderful feeling. It makes you think that here is somebody with whom you can relax, be yourself, and not play games. The fact that he seems to like you so much is very appealing. It encourages you to look at him in a more positive way. A typical woman's reaction: "I looked at him and saw all his faults right away, but he liked me so much that it made sense to me to compromise in terms of my ideal man—after all, what could be bad about being with somebody who totally adored me?"

His Agenda:

To this man, "special" and "forever" are two very different things. He does think you're special, and he wants very much for you to feel the same way about him. But that doesn't mean that he is thinking of anything past tomorrow morning.

The Smart Response:

Just because he doesn't seem to have any reservations about you doesn't mean that you shouldn't have some about him.

Now is the time to find out as much as possible about him, about his previous relationships, about his relationships with his family. Your judgment and acceptance of him should be based on the kind of man he is, not on his skill in manipulating your ego.

If your initial reaction to him was one of distrust, give it some thought and take it into consideration before you move forward.

3. He has a rocky history with women, but he makes you think he will be different with you.

Your Typical Response:

When you listen to him tell you about past relationships, you feel sorry for him. The way he presents his romantic failures makes you think that there was something wrong with the other women in his life. Perhaps they didn't love him enough. Perhaps he didn't like them as much as he likes you. Perhaps they were difficult and demanding. You believe it will be different with you because the two of you can share something special.

His Agenda:

When he tells you about problems in past relationships, it's his way of warning you not to get your expectations up too high. But he also doesn't want you to go away—so he has to explain why these relationships failed, as well as imply that it could be different with you. Often he is so out of touch with his problem that he really believes this.

The Smart Response:

■ If he has ever treated another woman badly, don't assume it's going to be different with you.

■ If he blames his past problems entirely on the woman, be skeptical.

■ If he blames his past problems on himself, he is probably telling the truth and will probably be the same with you.

His history is the most important information you have about him. Just because, at this point, he acts as if he will always be your best friend and strongest supporter, don't trust him until you have known him long enough and well enough to properly judge whether he can sustain any relationship for the long term.

4. He does everything he can to impress you: If he has money, he spends it; if he has special talents, he exhibits them; if he has "sensitivity" or "emotional depth," he reveals it.

Your Typical Response:

It's wonderful to have somebody treat you as though you are so special. You feel touched by the care he's taking to impress you. From your vantage point, it doesn't seem possible that a man would spend so much time and energy to win a woman unless he wanted her "forever," or close to it.

His Agenda:

Sure, he's trying to sell himself, but it's for the moment. He's not thinking about the future, but he will do whatever he can to win you over for the present. If he has money, you'll usually get gifts, or at the very least elaborate dinners and entertainment. If he doesn't, you'll probably get little pieces of his soul delivered in well-planned installments. If he has talents that he thinks you'll respond to, he'll let you know about them. Whatever skills he is using, chances are they are well-honed and have worked before.

Men are very aware of what they are doing here—very aware of the points they are making and how near they are to "closing" the deal. The wooing, the wining, the dining, the romance— it's all part of his here-and-now philosophy. He doesn't feel reluctant about sharing intimacies with a stranger because he isn't thinking of anything beyond selling himself.

The Smart Response:

This man does not think the way you do. "Special" now does not mean special forever—at least not to him. Enjoy the meals, enjoy the entertainment, but take it for what it is—not what you would like it to be. Keep this in mind, and don't be a quick sale. Let the buyer beware! He may be like the used-car salesman who pushes hardest because he knows he has a faulty product. Caution is the best strategy.

Use this time, before you commit yourself to anything, to get a more realistic view of him. Have him meet your friends. Meet his, and evaluate how he is with them and with the world. Make sure that there is room for you in his world, and that he's not hiding anything. If he acts as though he wants to exclude you or keep you separate from the rest of his life, better you should know it now.

It's easy to get swept away by this man's whirlwind courtship style, but you can't let this happen. If it is true love, there will be plenty more romance later—for the rest of your life, for that matter. *Make sure you've always got one foot on his brakes and another on yours.*

5. He appears vulnerable and acts as if he needs the relationship more than you do.

Your Typical Response:

He seems so needy that you almost feel sorry for him; you get the impression that he trusts you in a way that he trusts few people. You value his trust. His willingness to expose his vulnerability makes you feel it is safe for you to show yours.

His Agenda:

He *is* vulnerable and needy. If he's a true commitmentphobic, he spends so much of his time creating distance and running away that he rarely lets his defenses down. But at the very beginning of a relationship, before the woman wants a commitment from him, he feels safe, and all his emotional needs come pouring out.

The Smart Response:

Know that his vulnerability is deceptive, and that his willingness to expose it so quickly is suspect. Get more of the facts behind his feelings. If his version of his life seems too lopsided in his favor, watch out. His "sensitivity" to his problems does not mean he will be sensitive to yours. Regardless of whether or not you feel sorry for him, don't trust him to be equally empathetic with you. This early in the relationship, you should be far more protective of yourself. If he hasn't earned your trust, don't give it to him.

Even more important: Don't get so absorbed with his emotional needs that you establish a pattern of imbalance in the relationship (for example, acting as if he's the one with the problems, and you're the one who worries about them). Don't assume responsibility for his emotional well-being. Don't be so quick to bond. And don't feel sorry for him.

6. He indicates, either with words or with deeds, that he is looking for a meaningful, monogamous relationship, not just a superficial affair.

Your Typical Response:

You're happy to meet someone who seems to have such a solid value system. From everything he says, it seems fair to believe that once he meets the right woman, he is prepared to make a serious commitment. And from the way he looks at you, it seems equally fair to assume that, unless you do something wrong, you could be that woman.

His Agenda:

He's not trying to trick you. He truly means what he says. If he is a commitmentphobic, he has probably never had a *good* relationship, which is why he wants one so badly. But that doesn't mean that he is capable of developing such a relationship. Once again, he is expressing a fantasy need. When he talks about wanting a solid relationship, he is speaking in the general, not the specific. When he talks like this, he's not making promises. It doesn't occur to him that anyone might expect him to begin acting on his words immediately. He may be thinking about having this relationship the following year—or just some future "ultimately."

However, even though he doesn't want all the obligations that come with commitment, he wishes that he could have all the positive things that togetherness brings, not the least of which is the sense that the woman is there if he needs her to be there, whenever he feels like it.

The Smart Response:

Know that he doesn't think the way you do. Before saying the kinds of things that he says, you would weigh your words very carefully. Don't assume that he is doing the same thing.

Don't let his words encourage you to start thinking about

family and husband and the long term. Don't be so eager to believe in his sincerity that you get swept along. Think about it! A man who is genuinely interested in commitment probably wouldn't start talking about it so soon, and if he did it would probably be in the specific, not the general.

If he expresses traditional values, don't assume that he will place a greater value on a woman who has all the qualities of a perfect partner. *Most important*: Don't start trying to become the perfect woman/wife/mother figure in an effort to convince him that you're the woman he's looking for.

This is the time for you to remember that you are a smart, independent, emotionally secure woman who should be asserting her own sense of identity. Think objectively about what you truly want in a long-term, committed relationship. Are you sure this man could provide that, even if he wanted to? In other words, is he really right for you, or are you overlooking a lot because of what you perceive as the strength of his interest in you?

7. **He is willing to go out of his way to be with you and do things for you, breaking other plans, traversing great distances if necessary, etc.**

Your Typical Response:
Wow! Nothing is too much for him to do to please you. If he has to drive sixty miles each way to see you every night, it's no problem. Your kitchen ceiling needs plastering—no problem. It seems apparent to you that he's acting as though he's applying for the job of husband, and he's getting a near perfect score.

His Agenda:
At this moment, he's obsessed, the chase is on, his adrenaline is pumping, and nothing is too much. It's part manipulation and part hormones. He's genuinely excited and into the relationship, but he's thinking about today. He's not thinking about how this is being interpreted or whether he might be expected to continue acting this way.

The Smart Response:
You should take a closer look at him. Is he this way with his parents? Is he this way with friends? Does he go out of his way

for people in general? Is his behavior a reflection of his character, or is it just something he's doing now because he wants to cement the sale? Realize that many men who have a true sense of priorities might not be willing to drop everything for a woman so early in the relationship. If it happens after six months, it's one thing, but at the very beginning, it may be further proof of the unrealistic quality of his pursuit.

Sure, let him paint your apartment and drive excessive distances just to see your face—if that's what he wants to do. But don't assume a relationship has been established in which he will act like a husband.

More important, don't start acting like a wife because you assume that's what he wants from you. Don't start going out of your way to do "wifely" things.

And, if you haven't slept with him yet, don't do it just because he cleaned your garage, fixed your car, or washed your dog.

8. He phones all the time, often "just to say hello" or "just to hear your voice."

Your Typical Response:

He always seems to need to know that you're there for him. It makes you want to be there, and you tend to go out of your way to make sure that he can always reach you. After all, you tell yourself, I know he would want to be there for me. His "neediness" encourages you to believe that you could be equally dependent on him, if you should want to be.

His Agenda:

He *is* thinking about you all the time, albeit unrealistically, and he phones you when he thinks about you. At this stage he does want to know that you are there for him. It doesn't occur to him that you might interpret this to mean that you can count on him.

The Smart Response:

Pavlov had a little bell; these men have telephones. No woman ever feels as free about calling or not calling as any man. Consequently, knowing that this is an area where women can be easily manipulated, you should be going out of your way to keep him from "training" you with the phone.

Don't establish the habit of putting everything aside for his phone calls—if you miss his call, and he doesn't call back, it would have happened at some point anyway. Don't always leave a message that tells him where you are. Don't worry about whether he will become insecure if he can't find you at home. Don't talk to him on the phone at work any longer than you would any other friend. Don't miss your favorite television show, or leave your clothes stuck in the Laundromat, because you didn't want to tell him you were busy.

And, most importantly, don't think—even if he calls you five times a day—that this means that he wants to talk to you "forever."

9. He openly engages in "future talk," making plans for things the two of you will do together. He may even refer to the two of you as "we."

Your Typical Response:

It's really terrific to meet a man who doesn't seem to be afraid of planning ahead. You get the feeling that he's doing it because he wants you to feel as secure in the relationship as he would like to feel. A typical reaction: "Right away, he told me how much I would like his family's beach house. It made me think he planned for us to be together for a long time . . . I think I began to count on it."

His Agenda:

His concept of the future is different from yours. At this point, he is thinking about all the "ideal" moments he would like to spend with you without thinking about all the in-between hours—i.e., day-to-day life—one must go through to get to all these special times. He doesn't think he is promising anything and would be shocked if you tried to hold him to what he said at some future point. There is also an element of manipulation here. He knows a woman is going to respond positively to this kind of talk, and that she's going to think his interest in her is sincere. Even though it's a setup, in his head he thinks he is sincere, and he doesn't perceive the contradiction.

The Smart Response:

Don't let his talk of the future seduce you into thinking you are in a long-term, stable relationship. Don't start acting like a wife-figure here and overlook his flaws because of a casual reference to a future. Don't start planning dinner parties with him.

Since his references to a future make you think that he is trying to make you feel secure, the tendency is to spend even more time making sure he feels secure or comfortable in the relationship. This is a major mistake. His "we" does not mean what your "we" means.

Don't think about including him in your vacation plans or holiday plans until he realistically includes you in his. Don't start changing your life for him. If anything, this is the time to maintain your independence and your own life.

When he introduces you into all aspects of his life, then you can do the same with him—not before. When you meet his family, then he can meet yours, etc.

10. He acts as though you're a priority in his life.

Your Typical Response:
You make him *the* priority in your life, and when you think priority, you don't equivocate. He comes first—it's as simple as that.

His Agenda:
He doesn't think of words like *priority*. He is simply acting on impulse, with no thoughts about what his actions mean or how they will be interpreted.

The Smart Response:
You should be the number one priority in your life. Other priorities include your family, your children (if you have any), your friends, your career, your cat, your dog, and all the other things and people in your life that have earned priority status. At this stage of the relationship, don't make him more important than everybody else—and never make him more important than you!

11. He appears sensitive to women's issues and puts down other men who are thoughtless and unkind to women.

Your Typical Response:
You're really impressed! He seems so sensitive and aware. It's easy to think that he is never carelessly thoughtless or unkind

to women. He sounds so judgmental about men who behave otherwise that you are sure he will never behave that way.

His Agenda:

This is almost a method of making himself feel better about himself. He knows on some level that he is deceptive, and he needs to keep reassuring himself, and you, that he isn't as bad as other men. He thinks he is in touch with women's needs, and he doesn't think he is using you for sex. In short, he wants to believe he's a good guy.

The Smart Response:

A man who has hurt women in the past is sensitized and defensive about it. He's apt to notice more and be more judgmental about other men's behavior than a Dagwood Bumstead husband for whom these problems don't exist. Consider the possibility that what he says may be projection on his part, and that his "sensitivity" to women's issues is merely a means of masking his own rocky history and questionable intentions.

12. He does everything he can to convince you to trust him —and eventually you do.

Your Typical Response:

How could you not trust him? He says everything you want to hear. Also, it is so obvious that he trusts you. When you talk about trusting him, you mean long-term, permanent, best-friend/lover trust. It doesn't occur to you that he could mean something different.

His Agenda:

His concept of trust is probably different from yours. What many men mean when they say women can trust them is that they are not "using" women just for sex. (This definition seems so sophomoric that it doesn't even occur to the majority of women.)

The Smart Response:

Make sure you are both speaking the same language, and ask him to clarify his terms. Trust to him often has a distinctly temporary connotation. When he says trust, does he mean long-term? And when he says long-term, does he mean two weeks, or forever?

Until you are further along in the relationship, trust yourself, trust your instincts, and withhold that kind of special trust until he has really earned it.

13. He convinces you to make a commitment (emotional and/ or sexual) to him.

Your Typical Response:

Okay, you have been won over. If sex is the issue, you're ready to agree to it. If exclusivity is what he wants, you're his alone. If he wants to move in, get engaged, or get married, you'll do it. Your last bit of resistance is gone, and you're prepared to make whatever sort of commitment he wants.

You've given this some careful thought, and you know what you are doing. You know what commitment means, and you know what it is to accept another human being and to work on a relationship. You think he has given this the same thought you have. In other words, you think he thinks like you and knows what you know.

You're pleased, because you think that now he can relax, and you can relax. You are going ahead with what he wants, assuming that this is the beginning of the best part of your relationship. It doesn't cross your mind that this could be the beginning of the end.

His Agenda:

His fantasy has been completed. Now he has to deal with reality. He has no idea of the importance you place on the commitment you are giving him. Yet he couldn't rest until he felt he had secured it from you. Now that he has it, he doesn't know what to do with it. For a fleeting moment, he'll feel really good. Then it will dawn on him what he has done. Unless he is prepared to move forward, he will start wanting to back off.

The Smart Response:

This is a very tricky moment in the relationship. If he hasn't given every indication that he understands the full weight of what he has asked of you, don't jump in first.

You don't have to prove anything to him. You know what it means to make a commitment. Don't make the mistake of believing he has given his words and actions the same careful thought you have.

If you haven't slept with him and are about to do so, make sure that the sexual act means the same thing to him that it does to you—*before* it happens.

Although his pursuit may have convinced you that you have a place in his life, don't start thinking and acting with the loyalty and devotion of a wife. If he says he is also prepared to commit, he should be as deeply committed as you are, and you both should know precisely what is meant by that.

If there are any shady areas in his life, or in the way he has responded, don't go ahead with major commitments—such as marriage or living together. If, at the moment you made your commitment, you sensed a pulling back or hesitation on his part, don't go forward until you are absolutely certain that he knows what he is doing and can handle it.

Making a commitment of any kind should be one hundred percent mutual, and you should both know exactly what you are doing, who you are doing it with, and what it means.

And, even if he fulfills all of these requirements, and you are prepared to stop reading this book at this point, remember: Always maintain your independence, a sense of your own self, and a healthy concern for your own needs.

Chapter 9

THE MIDDLE OF
A COMMITMENTPHOBIC
RELATIONSHIP

THE MIDDLE

The Middle begins when the commitmentphobic wakes up from his "here and now" fantasy and realizes that not only do you want him, you are probably thinking long term.

During the Beginning, he was totally preoccupied with convincing the woman that he deserved her acceptance, her attention, and, often, her soul. Now, he's made the sale, and he's thinking about what that means. He knows he is wanted. He is secure in this feeling. Unfortunately, to him, to feel secure is to feel trapped; and to feel trapped is to feel anxious, if not downright panic-stricken.

In other words, the woman's acceptance of him has brought the relationship to another level. Where he once felt uncertain and insecure, he now feels confident and secure—secure enough, in fact, to begin evaluating her and questioning whether or not *he* wants this relationship for the long term. But the prospect of long-term is frightening and suddenly he is uncertain whether or not he can really handle it.

With this in mind, he begins to take the relationship backward instead of forward, using one or both of the following methods:

■ *Setting Boundaries*: Nothing can stifle the growth of a relationship more than artificial boundaries, and the commitmentphobic knows it. Not only do they prohibit growth, but they

171

drive the woman crazy. What some men do is to convey to the woman, no matter how long or how closely they are involved, that she will not be included in his plans for major holidays, vacations, family events, etc. Others get their message across by putting limitations on the amount of sequential time they will spend with the woman.

■ *Fault-Finding*: Instead of enjoying the relationship and letting the love grow, he begins to pick it and her apart. Where once he glorified the woman, now he magnifies her every little flaw and problem. He may start with the problems that can be solved—such as where she lives or her current economic status. Eventually, he concentrates mostly on those things about her that cannot be changed.

It goes without saying that if the relationship has reached the boundary or fault-finding stage, it's because he's involved. He likes the woman, is attracted to her, and probably loves her to the best of his ability. As a matter of fact, the thought of losing her throws him into a total tizzy. But when he feels the possibility of commitment looming larger and larger, the commitment-phobic often begins to resent the woman for evoking all of these intense feelings.

Eventually, he is in total conflict, and begins to test these feelings. He moves forward and experiences total anxiety, so he withdraws. The first few times he withdraws, he feels *some* relief at removing himself from the situation which made him anxious, but his predominant feeling is one of missing the woman. So he moves closer again. But every time he moves closer, the woman's expectations of a commitment grow. Knowing this, his terror accelerates. He is aware that, unless a miracle occurs, he is probably never going to be able to make a commitment, but he wants to make sure that he doesn't have to leave the relationship before he is ready. So he keeps withdrawing more and more. Eventually, his sense of relief at avoiding commitment is greater than his sense of loss.

In his head, his commitment-induced panic often overcomes any loyalty or sense of fairness to the woman. He may realize that he has encouraged her to expect more, but he tends to overlook this. Basically what he is thinking is that she is trying to trap him, and as much as he may enjoy her, like her, and even love her, he feels like a hunted animal. What is driving him is the need to get away.

You, the woman, have an entirely different mindset at this point. When the Middle starts, you are head over heels in love . . . finally. While he is magnifying all of your faults, you are busy downgrading all of his. A typical example: "He's not as smart as I'd like him to be, he's a little fat, he's a little balding, he's certainly not as rich as Fred, but he loves me, and therefore this is worth more than all the rest put together."

This marks an important shift in the power structure of the relationship. You have stopped doubting, and hence he has begun doubting. You think your total acceptance is making him feel secure. Not so—it is making him feel trapped.

You may, or may not, be thinking long term right now. But on some level you are probably hoping that it will work, and you are certainly doing everything you think is appropriate to help the relationship reach that goal.

Any woman who reaches this stage has a major problem: She is still relating as if the commitmentphobic is pursuing her. She did not expect an attitudinal shift. She has evaluated all of the things he did to make her feel secure and happy. She assumes he will continue doing these things, and she behaves as though he is doing them—even when he has stopped.

Even when he is behaving in a totally destructive manner, there is a tendency on the part of many women to expect the feelings he expressed in the Beginning to re-emerge and make everything right. No matter how destructive, hurtful, rejective, or downright mean the commitmentphobic becomes as he struggles to convince himself, and her, that he is not trapped, many women simply do not believe what is happening.

A woman's first reaction is to express her distress in non-threatening terms. After all, she doesn't think anything is wrong and is certain that when she expresses what she feels, the problem will be cleared up and everything will go back to normal. As time goes on and his negativity accelerates, her dissatisfaction magnifies, and she vocalizes it. Arguments heat up. She thinks she is trying to straighten things out; he thinks she is pressuring him to the point of non-endurance.

The commitmentphobic does not help the woman deal with reality; instead, no matter how clear the relationship is in his mind, he is typically giving her mixed messages that confuse her totally. For example, even if he has begun seeing another woman, he may continue to call regularly and give her excuses that she can accept—such as working late, family problems, or fatigue.

Believe it or not, he thinks he is being clear with these messages. For example, by setting boundaries and withdrawing he thinks he is making it clear that he isn't going to make a commitment to her. By continuing to tell her that he loves her and doesn't want to lose her, he thinks he is spelling out his conflict. The problem is the woman doesn't know which message to believe. So she believes the one she wants to believe. She also does everything she can to convince him that commitment is the way to go.

Because the woman has been programmed to behave in certain ways, she tends to fall back on a wifely mode of behavior —almost as if to prove that she is "good for him." She tolerates more and she excuses more. In short, she tries to love more. But every time she does this, he feels a noose being pulled around his very being. Why? Because no matter what he says, he fears these wifely qualities more than he loves them.

In the Middle, the key word for the commitmentphobic is *conflict*. For the woman, it's *confusion*. She doesn't know what is going on, and, more often than not, she doesn't properly evaluate his behavior. She trusts the bond that exists between them, and thinks that love will conquer all.

In the Middle, the woman has emotional leverage based on the fact that the man has developed a strong attachment to her and considerable affection for her. Even though he is conflicted, the negatives don't outweigh the positives . . . yet. If anything, the opposite is true. If a smart woman wants this relationship, and thinks the man is worth the trouble, she has to use this leverage to get the relationship back to the Beginning where it can be restructured so that it is healthy, mutually independent, spacious, and nonthreatening. If you are going to be successful with a commitmentphobic, you are going to have to get back to the way you were in the Beginning, when he wasn't that important to you and when you were busy and happy without him.

And don't say that a relationship always has to move forward. Think of it as a sickly plant. If you ever want it to grow again, you have to cut it back and replant it in different soil. If you just keep trying to water it, it will drown.

The Typical Pattern

1. He seems to be backing away, as though something is scaring him. He may not call as often, be as attentive, etc.

Your Typical Response:

By now you are, simply put, crazy about him. You don't have the foggiest notion that his conflict is beginning to emerge. As far as you're concerned, he still likes you as much as he did at the Beginning. If anything, you would expect him to feel more intensely about you, as, indeed, you do about him.

Totally unaware that there has been a shift in his attitude, you act as though he is the man who seemed, more than anything else, to need your love and acceptance. You're so busy giving him all the warmth and security he seemed to want that you don't properly recognize or evaluate the first clues that he is backing away.

As a matter of fact, if you sense a problem, you may misinterpret it and go overboard to give him an even greater sense of security, thereby intensifying his commitment anxieties.

His Agenda:

At almost the exact moment he wins you over, he starts feeling trapped by the notion of long term. The possible implications of that terrify him. He senses the first rumblings of commitment-phobia, and he doesn't like it. He knows he has encouraged you to expect more, but suddenly he's not sure if he wants to give more—or if he can. The intimacy of the relationship is closing in on him, his problem is emerging, and something is telling him to retreat. Now, instead of worrying about how to win you, it occurs to him that someday he may want to get away from you. He realizes that these thoughts would be regarded as strange to anyone who had seen how intently he pursued you. So he starts, almost unconsciously, to train you to expect less than he had originally promised. He is establishing the necessary groundwork should he want to make a complete exit.

The Smart Response:

Take the first clue that he is backing off as an indication that something could be seriously wrong.

Although your first instinct is to move closer, the more appropriate action is to move away. Know that your reassurance and acceptance will not alleviate his problem. Quite the opposite, it may be causing the problem. So don't work at being extra-giving, loving, attentive, etc. It's the wrong reaction.

Instead, evaluate what's happening, and don't try to kid yourself. Realize that you may be with a man who regards too much togetherness as a trap. You may want to try backing away yourself to see what happens. However, if you distance yourself and he responds with jealousy, take it for what it is. It doesn't necessarily mean he has long-range plans for the two of you.

If you think he is worth the trouble, you might want to try to let him know by your actions, not by your words, that even if he loves you, he will not be smothered by you.

Plan more activities on your own. Not activities to make him jealous, just stuff that gets you out of the house and makes it clear that you have a life of your own that you don't want to relinquish.

Do not, whatever you do, get clutchy. And do not, whatever you do, plan your life so that it revolves around him.

2. Where his intentions were once clear, his words and actions are now full of mixed messages.

Your Typical Response:

You listen to the messages you want to hear and don't pay much attention to the others. It's not that you don't hear it when he starts becoming negative, but you're so accustomed and conditioned to his positive acceptance that you don't give his negative messages the weight they deserve.

If you are like most women, you are totally in the acceptance mode, and you want to enjoy the positive feelings. As a matter of fact, you are probably listing all the things about this man that you like and rationalizing away all the negatives.

At this stage, you're typically thinking how lucky you are to have found this wonderful man who likes you so much. How could you believe that he is beginning to analyze you for flaws?

His Agenda:

He is genuinely confused. He likes you; he may even love you. He likes the fact that he can trust you and rely on your acceptance. And he doesn't want you to go away. But he knows that he may not be able to make a commitment. He also knows that if he tells you this, it will ruin the relationship, and he doesn't want this to happen. But he also doesn't want you to expect anything. So he chooses a neither here nor there way of conveying his feelings to you.

His mixed messages may play themselves out by his being different with you in different settings. For example: When you are home alone together, it is all passion and intimate warmth; when there is a real-world activity, particularly one that includes other people, he backs off, almost as if to deny what exists between you. To justify his doing this, he may ruminate on what he perceives as your shortcomings.

He may still think you are wonderful, but whenever he thinks about forever, you become a little bit less wonderful. His thinking goes something like this: "Sure she's wonderful enough for now, but is she wonderful enough for forever?" So he starts cataloging your pluses and your minuses. An amazing and on-going debate begins to take place in his head as he argues with himself about whether he should or should not consider marrying you.

The only problem is that when he begins to think that you may be the "one" for him, instead of moving forward with that thought, he debates it, and the commitmentphobic in him starts coming up with reasons why you may be "wrong" or why it might not work.

In other words, he is a confused man giving confused messages.

The Smart Response:

You have to make sure you are listening to both messages. You can't just hear his messages of love and pretend that the others are not taking place.

In your mind, time with him is time with him, be it in bed

or at a party. Understand that in his mind, there is fantasy time, which includes passion and sex, and reality time, which includes day-to-day activities such as doing the laundry.

Even when a woman senses this difference, the tendency is to think that warmth and closeness will eventually win out. By what she does—intimate dinners, evenings at home, etc.—she stresses this side of the relationship. She thinks she is fanning the fires of love when in reality she is fanning the fear.

If this is happening, it may be time to evaluate the depth of his fear. Ask him. Is he worried about having to make a commitment? How about setting up a time frame during which you both agree not to think about the possibility of commitment? At the end of that time, you can both evaluate the relationship and tell each other honestly what each of you is feeling.

The most important thing here is that you don't allow the duality to become a permanent pattern. If he has substantial fears, you both had better know about them. That way you can decide for yourself how much of a risk you think he is.

Recognition enables you to protect yourself.

3. He makes it clear that certain important parts of his life, such as friends, family, or work, are "forbidden zones," and he excludes you from one or more of them. He often has seemingly plausible excuses for doing this.

Your Typical Response:

Of course you are hurt. As a matter of fact, you feel like an unpopular teenager being cut out of a high-school clique. But you don't know what to do about it. You think your relationship is based on intimacy and trust. Because of this, you don't want to demand that he include you. A worse thought: You're not sure that he would. You can't believe that this man could be so cruel. You don't understand it. So you look for someone else to blame. A typical reaction: "I believed him when he said his family was impossible. I thought he was afraid of them and wanted to protect me. I blamed them. I didn't want to believe that he just didn't want them to meet me. Then I realized that I had never met any of the people he worked with. I decided he must be ashamed of me. At first I was hurt, then I was very angry."

His Agenda:

He is clearly trying to limit your involvement in his life. He doesn't want you to become so entangled with everything he does that there is no escaping you. He realizes he is being hurtful—hence the excuses rather than the truth. On some level he knows that his behavior is chipping away at your ego, but this awareness doesn't overcome the anxiety he feels at the thought of including you in all aspects of his life.

In a peculiar way, by trying to let you know that there will always be boundaries that he doesn't want you to cross, the commitmentphobic in him is warning you to watch out. He doesn't want you to have unrealistic expectations of him.

The Smart Response:

If you have reached this point in a relationship, you're in trouble. Deal with it before it gets worse. If he is purposely being this hurtful, believe that he knows what he is doing. Basically, there are no excuses for this much emotional cruelty. Don't play his game by accepting *his*.

Think about it: What would you do if a friend did this to you?

Your responses should be appropriate to what is going on. But realize that *his* responses are not going to be what you want. If you tell him you're hurt, chances are he will think you are somehow trying to trap him. If he is the person who is causing you pain, don't turn to him to make the pain better.

Your attitude should depend somewhat upon the degree to which he is excluding you. If he's simply slow in introducing you to friends, but you can see he's making an effort, it's one thing. If he's actually engaging in hurtful behavior—not taking you with him for holiday dinners or major social events or treating you in a shabby fashion—you have to back off.

Notice what he is doing. Understand and accept what it means and respond in a similar but not punitive fashion. Know what boundaries mean. Don't try to cross his—but put up some strong ones of your own. If he continues to exclude you, you have to withdraw, perhaps totally. You can't allow yourself to be treated this way.

4. He is wary of events that include your family and friends, and avoids spending any serious time with these people.

It's as though he is sure that somebody there knows the truth about him, and it is not good.

Your Typical Response:

You want to share the good things in your life with him. You want him to like the people you like and love the people you love. But instead of looking forward to meeting and being with your family and close friends, he seems to want to avoid them. When he is at these events, he appears tense and nothing like the way he is when you're alone. In some instances, you may blame a friend or someone in your family for making him uncomfortable; you decide that this person either doesn't understand him or is jealous of him.

His Agenda:

The commitmentphobic is definitely uncomfortable at these events. When he's alone with you in a secluded, intimate setting, he can fool himself, but when he's with your family, he feels like an impostor. He thinks "deception" is written all over his face. You see, he feels that these people expect him to marry you. He may even feel as though he should be marrying you. He doesn't think he should be there unless he's prepared to make a commitment . . . and he's not.

The Smart Response:

Recognize that your family and friends may have a much better read on the situation than you do. They've known you a long time, and even when you don't get along, they feel an intense loyalty to you. Don't start thinking that nobody loves him and nobody understands him but you.

Don't detach yourself from your family and friends as a sign of loyalty to him—the "you and me against the world" syndrome. He's not Romeo, and you're not Juliet.

5. He treats you as though you are less of a priority and has a million excuses why.

Your Typical Response:

You don't immediately notice the change—the way he was at the Beginning left such an impression that your reactions are still based on the way he was, not on the way he is becoming.

Then, when you do notice, you go along with his explanations. If he says he is busier at work, you take him at his word. If he has a million and one things he has to do, or friends he has to see, you think the relationship is settling down into a normal day-to-day pattern, almost like a marriage. For a short time, you may even think it is nice that he is able to take you for granted. You think it means you will be able to do the same with him. You definitely don't think that his feelings are any different.

You believe him when he says his shift is temporary. So you feel sorry he has to work so hard, wait for his phone calls, and surprise him with late dinners, or special treats.

His Agenda:

You *have* become less of a priority, and he wants you to be aware of it—but not so aware of it that the relationship is threatened. Consequently, he makes up excuses and hopes you will give him distance, while you stay the same.

It doesn't occur to him that his excuses are giving you the rationalizations you need to act like a dutiful wife.

Here's how this works: He had been seeing you every Friday, Saturday, and Sunday, but now he only wants to see you Saturday. So he tells you he has to work, and he phones you, perhaps several times, on Friday night, and even on Sunday. He's not sure exactly what he wants to happen, but he is sure that he needs distance, and he's trying to set up a pattern which gives him more time away from you. Another scenario: Instead of coming over at six and having dinner, he finds excuses and doesn't show up until ten.

The Smart Response:

Don't think his behavior is temporary. He is not your husband of long standing with years of credit built up. This is not a man who has built gradually to a secure relationship. This is a man who you thought promised everything and is now withdrawing. If you want to continue past this point, know you have problems.

Stop acting like an understanding wife. Don't be there every time he calls or finds time for you. I'm not suggesting you play games. But I am telling you to lead your own life. If he's not making you a priority, don't make him one. And don't worry that he will think less of you for it.

It's totally inappropriate for you to send little baskets of food, or cute cards, or anything else to prove to him that you love him while he is working.

Don't make dinner for him and keep it warm for hours. As a matter of fact, don't do anything unless you are asked to do it. Once the relationship has reached this stage, the typical commitmentphobic feels too guilty to ask anything of a woman because he doesn't want her to ask too much of him. So if he's *asking* you to cook for him and wait up for him, he's probably sincere.

I understand that emergencies can arise at work, and people have genuine excuses, but a smart woman can usually make the distinction. You know when a man is just making excuses. You may not want to face it, but you know.

6. His sexual pattern changes, and he subtly may be turning you into the aggressor.

Your Typical Response:

When your man's sexual pattern changes, you notice it immediately. Typically your reactions vary: a part of you hopes that this is just a normal phenomenon that occurs when a relationship becomes more stable; another part of you is subtly trying to seduce him. If his changed behavior continues, you feel very rejected and worry that something about you is turning him off.

His Agenda:

In his mind, just as in yours, what could cement a relationship more than sexual intimacy? Therefore he thinks that showing an excess of sexual interest is somehow leading you on. For that reason, he has to do something in this area to let you know he is cooling down. Some men, for example, just change styles. Where once it was all romance, now it's all technique.

Many others, however, feel every bit as romantic—what they do is back off and stop assuming the initiative. Remember the Beginning, when he was prepared to assume responsibility for unbuttoning every little button, not to mention turning off the lights and locking the door? Now he does the opposite. It's not that he's exactly the reluctant lover. He just doesn't want to take responsibility for sex, because to him that means taking responsibility for the continuation of the relationship. If you do most of the initiating, then he can say it was your idea, and he, of course, doesn't have to feel guilty for continuing to "lead you on."

The Smart Response:

The first thing to know is that you have to deal with reality. If he's cooling down, he's cooling down. And it's emotional. Don't assume responsibility for the sex, and don't think that the sex will somehow bond the two of you.

It's natural for you to feel rejected and insecure. But don't try to change what's happening by suddenly becoming more seductive. Don't wrap yourself in Saran Wrap and meet him at the door. The bond between you will not get stronger every time you get him into bed. Remember, the bond is what is scaring him.

Don't assume responsibility for anything sexual—no romantic dinners, no flimsy (or edible) garments for him to tear off or digest, etc. It's not that he's suddenly lost interest in you—it's that sex represents one of the strongest ties between the two of you. This fact is a signal for you to be more sexually cautious, not more sexually aggressive.

Don't worry that if you back off sexually, he'll start sleeping with someone else. If he's going to do it, he's going to do it. Besides, a hard-core commitmentphobic is more likely to want to sleep with another woman precisely because he *is* sleeping with you.

Do not hang over him with affection, touching, stroking, nibbling. (The impulse is understandable—there was so much sexual intimacy between you that it stands to reason that you don't understand why it has changed.) And don't read magazine articles that tell you how to turn your man on.

So what should you do? Shift your focus away from the sex. Just forget about it for a while. Say you're tired and go to bed, and sleep, before he does. Keep distancing yourself subtly—don't hang on his arm or by his side. Then, when he gets interested again, don't sleep with him just because he's finally in the mood and you think you should be. Let him woo you all over again. And if distancing yourself works, whatever else you do, don't point it out to him.

MOST IMPORTANT! Don't feel rejected; there is nothing wrong with *you*.

7. **He establishes a definite schedule of when and how he has time for you—on his terms—and always seems to have other demands that have to be met first; by definition, this disturbs the natural flow of a relationship.**

Your Typical Response:

You get the sense that unless you adjust your life to fit around his schedule, he would have no time for you. So you adapt, but his "rules" upset you. They are unfair and make the relationship feel very unequal. Also, they destroy spontaneity and disrupt the natural flow of a relationship. The whole situation leaves you feeling frustrated and demoralized.

By now, he is so different than he was at the Beginning that you don't know what to do about it. Typically you look for more ways to please him, thinking that he will notice how hard you are trying to make him happy. You hope that this will work and that he will again become the loving man you remember.

His Agenda:

He doesn't want the relationship to have a natural flow, so he purposely places boundaries on it. The way he schedules time is one of the more telling indications that he is placing restrictions. Since he is in charge of the scheduling, he is guaranteeing himself boundaries that only he can cross, if and when he wants.

Some clear indications that a man is placing boundaries:

■ He sees you every Saturday night, but come Sunday morning, he is always out the door by 10 A.M. and never, ever lingers.

■ He will never plan a vacation or a long weekend with you.

■ He disappears on holidays.

■ He never spends unstructured time with you.

The Smart Response:

This is simple. Don't adjust your schedule to meet his schedule. When you twist yourself into a pretzel for him, he can't help but notice it. Don't act like a dutiful wife who is always home for her husband. It makes him feel more threatened. To him, rightly, it indicates that you are thinking long term. Don't fight with him about his schedule. But do start making your own plans. Don't threaten, by the way, or point out what you're doing. Just take care of yourself. I'm not telling you to engage in manipulative behavior that will play upon his insecurities and force him to behave differently. I'm just telling you to get genuinely busy and stop doing all the accommodating.

Don't try to get him to spend more time with you by taking the initiative and asking him out. Typically, under these conditions he will either say no and make you feel miserable, or he will say yes and look so unhappy for the entire evening that you will still end up feeling miserable.

Obviously, some men are more extreme about boundaries than others. I spoke to one woman who told me that for three years she and her boyfriend had spent only Wednesday and Saturday nights together. For three years, he had never once allowed her to linger for even a moment on Sunday. Every week he said he had to see his kids, and he would jump out of bed by eight, take her to a local diner for breakfast, and drive her home. Well, one Sunday when they woke up, a blizzard was taking place outside. He still insisted that she had to get home, even though the roads were not plowed, the diner wasn't open, and there was no way to get anywhere.

The point of this story is that many women allow these restrictions to be placed on the relationship because they convince themselves that there is a real reason for the time boundary. But more often than not, he is intentionally making you feel this way to insure himself that he has the freedom to walk into your life as he desires, but that you don't have equal rights in his. No relationship can sustain this kind of inequality.

8. He treats most of your requests as though they are demands and seems to resent being "counted on." He indicates he resents "expectations," though he doesn't make it clear what these expectations are.

Your Typical Response:
You probably start acting as though you are walking on eggshells, tying superhard not to make any demands on him. You

want to make him happy, but you're beginning to feel that you are doing all of the adjusting.

You also remember the way he was at the Beginning, when he would do anything for you. You think that is the way he is normally, and his current behavior is temporary. You may start trying to talk to him about his mother and the demands you are sure she placed on him during what you imagine to be his tortured childhood.

There is a tendency to believe that if you do more for him, he will do more for you, so you bend over backward not to withhold anything from him.

His Agenda:

He is hypersensitive to anything that might be construed as an invitation to make you dependent on him. He thinks that if he does anything for you, you will expect still more, and it will become harder and harder to get out. He doesn't want you to count on him, like you would if he were your husband. For example: If he goes to the store for you, he's a husband. If he plans a dinner party, or helps you hang a painting, he's a husband. If he goes with you to your cousin's wedding, he's a husband.

He also doesn't want you to remember the way he was at the Beginning when he would do almost anything you asked.

The Smart Response:

Forget about the Beginning of the relationship and don't assume that he has the same intentions as the man who willingly painted your kitchen, drove you to the doctor, and picked you up from work when it got cold. He's not the same, and he wants to forget that phase.

Don't start doing more for him in the hope that he will get the message and respond in kind. Don't make excuses for his behavior. Get it through your head that his behavior is not a test—he is not acting this way because he doesn't want a woman to "take advantage of his good nature." He's acting this way because he doesn't want to be a husband. So don't act like a wife. And don't start fighting with him, like a wife, about the way he is treating you.

You see, the chances are that you are both interpreting the relationship the same way. He thinks that if he allows you to become dependent, he will immediately turn into your husband. You think that if you can get him to fulfill just one or two small demands, he will see that it's not so terrible, and he will be less resistant to becoming your husband.

Just forget this kind of tug-of-war, and don't ask anything of him. For example: If you have carpentry that you want done, either hire a handyman or learn how to use power tools yourself. If you have a party for which you need an escort, ask a friend. The commitmentphobic doesn't think the way you do, and he doesn't want what you want. So don't worry that you'll be making him feel insecure or unnecessarily jealous.

If your independent stance makes him turn around and alter his behavior, perhaps you can work on building a relationship with different ground rules.

In the meantime, ask yourself why you are putting up with a relationship in which you are getting so little, simply because of a few golden weeks at the Beginning.

9. He doesn't seem to "hear" what you are saying and seems to be paying less and less attention to your needs.

Your Typical Response:

You pay more and more attention to everything he says, dissecting and analyzing it in your mind. Usually, you spend a great deal of time talking about it with friends. It's possible that you may even consider therapy—just so you can talk about him with a professional.

What happened? In the Beginning, he made you feel as though you had finally found the perfect combination of lover and best friend. Now, he doesn't want to discuss anything—least of all the problems in the relationship. He almost ignores your requests, and acts as if he doesn't care whether you are sad or glad.

You think something must have gone wrong that you know nothing about, and you wonder if there is some sort of massive misunderstanding taking place. Consequently you try to get more insight into what he might be going through.

Because he won't talk to you about what's happening, you have long conversations with him in your head in which you try out different approaches and defend yourself.

Sometimes you think that he will learn by example, so you do everything you can to discuss his problems with him and to be more understanding and more supportive of him, his motivations, and his psychology.

In other words, you do everything possible to try to figure out *what is going on!*

His Agenda:

In his head, he's phasing you out. In the Beginning, paying attention was one of his ways to show you how much he cared. Now, not paying attention is his way of showing you that he is afraid to care. It's not a question of priorities. It's not that he has other more important things on his mind taking all of his attention. It's that he doesn't want to hear what you are saying. As a matter of fact, he hears it—he knows you are unhappy. You don't have to convince him that you are wonderful; he knows you're wonderful. This is not the problem. The problem is that he is pulling away. Not paying attention to what you say is just one of the ways he does it. He is tuning you out.

The Smart Response:

Don't make listening to him or talking about him your primary activity. Force yourself to stop having endless discussions with friends about *his* problem. Don't allow thinking about him, or the problem, to become an obsession.

Don't start having lengthy discussions with him about his problem, either. You are not his therapist, and you are not his mother. Regardless of how much, or how little, you understand his problem, it's not your job to work it out for him.

Erase from your head all romance-novel fantasies that tell you that he will eventually come to his senses and throw himself at your feet.

Every time he fails to pay attention to your needs, don't immediately respond by doing something especially attentive for him in the hope that if he realizes how much you love him, he will change his behavior. Once again, he is not testing you to see whether or not your love can withstand all. He knows how much you love him—that's a big part of the problem.

Instead of concerning yourself with his problems, worry about your own happiness and about getting insight into whether or not you should give up on this man and get on with your life.

10. He praises you for being loyal, devoted, intelligent, a good cook, understanding—all "wifelike" qualities—but they simultaneously seem to make him uncomfortable.

Your Typical Response:

He tells you he respects you for your honesty and your loyalty, and you try to be even more honest and loyal. He tells you he admires your solid traditional values, and you articulate values that are even more solid and more traditional. He tells you he respects your intelligence, and you leave your most brutally esoteric books lying casually on your coffee table. He says he is really happy that you share the same taste in music, and every time he walks through the door, he is greeted by the sound of your stereo. He always compliments you on your cooking, and you invest in a Cuisinart.

In other words, you assume the man knows what he is saying and places a value on the qualities he compliments. You want to please him, and, unfortunately, to prove yourself to him, so you emphasize the aspects of your personality he says he admires.

His Agenda:

Basically, he compliments you on all qualities that make him feel trapped. These are qualities that he thinks a good wife should have, and he also thinks he should appreciate them more. When he compliments you this way, it is almost as if he is arguing with himself. He is supposed to want all the things you represent—so why doesn't he?

What he is thinking is, "You'd make a great wife—but I'm not sure I want a wife." Make no mistake about it, he really likes these qualities, but they make him uncomfortable because they remind him too much of the "M" word.

The Smart Response:

Don't take his words to mean that you should start cooking more, be more understanding, or in any other way, shape, or form try to move closer to the "ideal" wife-figure he has in mind.

Don't assume that these are genuine compliments and that you should go on acting accordingly. This is a mistake. If you don't believe me, think about the women who have lasted in his life. Do any of them have these qualities? I say this because so many men who claim to want all these wonderful "wifely" things ultimately end up with women whose idea of home cooking is to ask the man to bring home the Chinese food.

11. **He begins to find problems associated with seeing you. For example: He can "never find parking near your house." He has "trouble sleeping in your bed." You "live too far away." He is "allergic to your cat."**

Your Typical Response:

You find yourself saying, "I'm sorry," for no reason and start trying to adapt your environment to suit his needs. When the two of you first met, he didn't find it so difficult to see you. Is it possible, you wonder, that he's telling you to buy a new bed, move to a more convenient location, or put your cat up for adoption?

His Agenda:

He, also, knows that these things were not a problem before. He fully realizes that if it was the bed, and if he had long-range plans for sharing one with you, something could be done about buying a new mattress. All these complaints do is help him find rationalizations and excuses for not spending as much time with you. He doesn't want to tell you that he's having trouble with the relationship, so he tells you about the parking. He doesn't want to find solutions for any of these problems, and chances are that if you were to find solutions, he would simply come up with more, different, and often much more complicated reasons why seeing you is sometimes difficult.

The Smart Response:

Absolutely do not adapt your environment to suit his needs. Do not offer to get a new bed or give your cat to a friend. These problems are not real and should not be treated as though they are. If you question what I'm saying, try to find a solution for one of his complaints and see what happens.

I know a woman whose boyfriend complained bitterly about

the bed. So she went out and bought a new bed. Unfortunately, he never slept in it because he suddenly decided it had not been the bed that had kept him from sleeping. It was her quilt—he was allergic to her quilt, and he sat up all night rubbing his eyes until they were red and puffy.

This is extreme, but it's a good example of the fact that you will not win by trying to adapt your environment to fit his needs until after the wedding—and even then this should always be a joint effort.

If he can't sleep, tell him to go home. If he has trouble parking, tell him not to bother coming over. If he is allergic to your cat, meet at his apartment and let him make dinner.

Sometimes a man doesn't become this way until after he has moved in. Then, he has a million and one problems associated with where the two of you are living—but he makes it sound as if you are responsible for all of them. In that case, let him take all the responsibility for making changes. If he needs a new bed, for example, let him choose it and arrange to have it delivered.

If you are already married or living together, observe this tendency to find fault with your environment carefully. Some of his complaints may reflect small adjustments that have to be made in any relationship, or they could be indicative of a larger problem that is going to grow. You can test this by changing one or two things to suit his needs, and then see whether or not his list of problems gets shorter or longer. If he settles down, terrific. But if he finds new things to complain about, understand what this may mean for the future.

Whatever you do, don't become defensive or guilty when he complains about your refrigerator, garbage container, medicine chest, etc. Don't assume all the responsibility for changing things. Instead, let him initiate the changes that are important to him.

12. **He starts to find fault with you and looks for reasons why the relationship will not work. He may hurt you by bringing these "faults" to your attention, particularly if they are things you can't change (e.g., "I'm not sure if my parents can ever accept the fact that you are one of the following: Irish, Italian, black, white, Jewish, Gentile, Wasp, short, tall, divorced, too old, too young,**

too rich, too poor, too medium)." Or he may save them up and spring them on you when he finally decides the relationship should end. (Incidentally, these "faults" rarely have anything to do with anything you have done to him; they almost always have to do with the "way you are." He was fully aware of these qualities when he entered the relationship and persuaded you to join him.)

Your Typical Response:

When he first starts this sort of thing, it sounds like a joke, and you're mildly amused. Then you become terribly defensive and hurt. You can't believe that he is saying this sort of thing to you. Ultimately, you are furious.

His Agenda:

He fully realizes that some of these qualities were what attracted him to you in the first place. But he also knows that these were built-in excuses to help him get out of the relationship when it came to commitment time. These built-in "faults" are the strongest escape routes out of a relationship since they cannot be changed. He knows you can get a new bed, lose weight, gain weight, or change the color of your hair. But you can't change your religion, your height, your age, your ethnic background, or your parents' economic status. When he starts pointing these problems out to you, it does not mean that he's leaving . . . yet. It just means he wants you to know he has a "legitimate" reason to do so, should he want to. He doesn't feel comfortable until he's brought them to your attention. When you know about them, he thinks he's made it clear to you that he may eventually have to leave you.

These "faults" are often a way of blaming someone else for the possible eventual demise of the relationship. He will use his parents, his lawyer, and his children from a previous marriage as excuses to get out of something with you, in the same way he used his parents when he was a little kid. In other words, he can't marry you because Mommy and Daddy won't let him.

The Smart Response:

Know that you are dealing with a jerk. Making someone else feel awful about something she can't change is just rotten. If it bothered him that much, he should never have gotten involved with you. You know it, and he should know it. Don't defend your height, or your ethnic or religious background.

I know it's hard to believe that this man who seemed to like you so much is now being so shabby. Believe it, and back away. Don't turn to him as though he is going to be able to protect you from this part of himself. You're right in thinking that he doesn't really mean what he's saying, but that doesn't mean that he may not act on it.

When a normally sensitive man indulges in this kind of cruel and thoughtless "fault" finding, chances are he is so overwhelmed by the intensity of his commitmentphobic anxiety that he simply cannot stop what he is doing. He wants to drive you away, and that is precisely what is happening.

He doesn't want to hurt you. But he *is* hurting you, and that's the reality you should be dealing with. It's vitally important to your mental health that you stay realistic and don't resort to living in a fantasy land in which you expect him to apologize for being such a creep and go back to the way he was at the Beginning.

Once again, the best thing you can do is to limit his involvement in your life and your involvement in his life and don't expect a miracle to change him.

13. **He may start leaving clues that he is looking at, thinking about, or actually seeing another woman. (Often it is a woman from his past.)**

Your Typical Response:
You may begin finding things that indicate another woman has been in his apartment. Or you might catch him in an outright lie. When this happens, it usually catches you off-guard. You didn't expect it. You may have worried about it, but you thought that he was too involved with you. You thought the love you shared was real. It doesn't make any sense to you. As a matter of fact, considering the kinds of things he has said to you, it seems downright unbelievable. You probably confront him, hoping against hope that he will deny it.

His Agenda:

A worst-case commitmentphobic usually uses another woman as the final straw in a relationship. Typically, he doesn't want to be in a committed relationship with this woman any more than he does with you. But her presence reassures him that he has a way out of his involvement with you.

Sometimes this happens just as the relationship seems about to move to another stage. Perhaps you were planning to live together. Perhaps you were even talking about marriage.

Often, because he hasn't had time to meet anyone new, he pulls in a woman he's known before—sometimes it's a "repeater" from his past, a Lazarus-like ex-wife or girlfriend who is resurrected whenever necessary.

If he's actually seeing another woman, don't take it lightly. It's a clear indication, no matter what he says, that he is on his way out. He simply can no longer be with you and be comfortable. Something about the relationship has progressed to the point where it can't continue the way it was.

He is sometimes so commitmentphobic by this point that he can't properly evaluate you, his feelings for you, or your feelings for him. He may see everything you do as a means of manipulating him into a commitment. If you make a nice dinner, he thinks you're trying to trap him; if you buy him a present, he thinks you're trying to trap him; if you are especially attentive, he thinks you're trying to trap him; if you do anything to make him jealous, he thinks you are using his jealousy to trap him.

Going out with other women is his way of not feeling trapped. And when he starts letting you know that he's doing it, it is often his way of spelling out that he won't be making a commitment to you.

But believe it or not, he's still not sure in his own head that he is leaving.

The Smart Response:

What should you do? First, if you are a perceptive woman without a history of over-reacting, believe the clues. Confronting him will accomplish nothing because he will probably deny it. If you have reached this point, the relationship is probably out of control. What you need, more than anything else, is a vacation from him and from the way he is making you feel.

Here's a list of do's and don'ts to follow.

- Do retreat as far back as you can comfortably go.
- Don't phone him to check on his whereabouts.
- Do start thinking about your future with other men.
- Don't start thinking that you did something wrong.
- Don't start questioning your judgment.
- Don't start going through his belongings, papers, or phone bills looking for more evidence.
- Don't assume that this is just a little something he's going through that is going to pass.
- Do find something else to think about—anything. Some possible suggestions: Join a health club and use it regularly. Go back to school. See every movie. Call all your old friends. Make dinner dates with anyone you can think of and don't spend the evening talking about him. Take a vacation.
- Don't start doing more things for him.
- Don't try to intensify your sexual involvement as though that will ward off competition—it won't.
- Don't start trying to prove to him that you are better, smarter, sexier, etc. than any other woman.
- Do stay off the phone with him.

At this point, the most important thing is that you retain your sense of self and don't start wallowing in feelings of rejection. If you do they can get out of hand, and you will feel that he is the only person who can make you feel better. Thinking this way can lead to a major depression. So don't do it.

Remember, he will regard anything you do to make yourself more appealing—including catering to his ego—as a way of manipulating him into making a commitment.

I think the only thing you can do at this point is to walk away for a while, regain emotional control, and carefully evaluate his reactions.

14. If he has been seeing another woman, he lies about it or plays it down, continuing to assure you that you are the most important person in his life.

Your Typical Response:

You don't really believe him when he lies, but you want to. Basically you are so relieved by his assurances that you disregard the facts and the evidence. He either indicates or tells you that you're the most important woman in his life, and that's all that matters to you. But you're feeling very wary, very anxious, very insecure, and very disturbed.

His Agenda:

He lies to you because he figures that to admit anything would end it with you—which is something, believe it or not, he still isn't sure he wants to do. I don't think he is even considering how unhappy this is making you. He is obsessed with his own fear and his own problem. Once again, this is worst-case commitmentphobic behavior. All he is trying to do, on all levels of consciousness, is tell you he can't make a permanent commitment to you now . . . and possibly ever.

The Smart Response:

The best thing you can do is to remove yourself physically from his immediate environment. Don't believe his lies, excuses, or explanations—but don't argue with him, either. If he's a genuine commitmentphobic, you know why he's lying, and you understand that anything you do will intensify his commitment-phobic anxiety.

If another woman is involved, ignore the immediate impulse to move in closer so you can't be displaced. This is not sensible behavior. If he's acting out with other women, he is being so hurtful that you really should evaluate whether or not you can afford to take this sort of emotional beating. For this reason, you should withdraw and think about yourself. If you insist that you still love him and want to be with him, then you should still withdraw and think about yourself because that's the only way in which the relationship stands a chance.

Don't be relieved that he cares enough about you to take the time to lie. What's at issue here is not the depth of his feelings for you. The problem is that he doesn't know what to do with those feelings, and there's a good possibility that if he is the kind of man who uses other women to extricate himself from the terrors of commitmentphobia, he will never be able to make a solid, sincere commitment to anyone. You have to deal with the reality of what he is doing, and what he is capable of doing.

Don't, for heaven's sake, think this is something the two of you can work on together. Closeness is what is causing the problem. More closeness will not alleviate it; usually it makes it worse. The key word for you is *withdraw.*

Many of the women I spoke to said that when a relationship reached this point, they became almost obsessed with the man's behavior. Several told me that they thought he was having a mental breakdown, and they tried to behave like loving, long-term wives, standing by their mates. Needless to say, this did not work.

15. He is obviously deeply conflicted, and may respond to your threats to end the relationship by promising to change; he may even cry.

Your Typical Response:

If he gets upset when you threaten not to see him again, you breathe a sigh of relief and think he finally "woke up." He promises to change, and you believe him. He may even cry, and you're sincerely touched. What typically happens at this point is that you go back to behaving exactly as you did before. Within hours, you are all love and acceptance.

His Agenda:

If you try to end the relationship at this point, even he is surprised by how shocked and hurt he is. Obviously his attempts to distance himself worked all too well, and he finds himself being removed from a relationship he's not yet ready to leave. Remember, he does have very strong feelings for you. He wants you to be there—he just doesn't want you to be there, if you know what I mean.

So he promises to change—he's so moved he may even cry. But even as he's saying it, he knows that he probably won't be able to follow through on his promises. He does not give you specific ways in which he will change; he just promises to try.

The Smart Response:

This is a great opportunity to make some real changes in the relationship, but you have to be prepared to back off and behave differently. You can agree to date him, with restrictions, if he agrees to couples counseling. I don't think you will be able to make the kind of major step-by-step changes that are necessary without outside help, and the sooner you get it, the better. Incidentally, if you genuinely want the relationship to continue, I think it's a mistake to substitute individual therapy as a means of saving the relationship. It probably won't be able to accomplish the sort of immediate improvements that the relationship must have if it is to continue. Individual therapy may be called for in addition to couples counseling.

If you can't afford couples therapy, see if you can get premarital or couples counseling through your religious group. If he can commit himself to going with you to some outside person, you have a better chance of resolving your problems.

Whatever you do, don't be relieved by his promises to change if it isn't clear to both of you specifically *how* he plans to change. A vague, "I'll try," is not enough. He needs as much help with this as you do. If you immediately let things resume the way they were, the chance of sliding back is too great.

You are right in thinking that the man who cries and promises to change is vulnerable—at this point—but this vulnerability won't last. So make the most of it.

Some things to remember: Don't feel sorry for him. Don't expect him to make all the changes—you have to change, too, by becoming more independent and less clutchy. Don't expect him to stop feeling frightened and start making commitments that will last without help. Don't think he's a big, strong man who will be able to take control and do what's necessary.

You have a real edge here. Use it to make positive changes in the relationship.

16. Despite everything he says, nothing ever changes; he doesn't allow the relationship to grow or progress and he won't talk about it.

Your Typical Response:

You may not insist upon a total commitment, but you want some show of good faith; you want to know you're not wasting your time, and you want things to get better. You can no longer handle his "It's not that I don't care for you" speech.

You have a list of things you want to talk to him about. They include:

- How he can be so hurtful if he says he cares about you?
- Will he ever be ready to make a commitment?
- Is he ever going to arrange his life so that you are a priority?
- Why does he keep leading you on if nothing is going to happen?
- Why does he exclude you from other parts of his life?
- Why won't he give you the place in his life that you deserve?

It doesn't matter whether you try calm conversation, hysterical sobbing, or out-of-control screaming; he won't discuss what's happening, and he won't do anything. You're sure he cares for you, but it's not enough. You don't understand how anyone can be so stubborn. You decide he's being self-destructive.

You try to get him to enter therapy or talks to someone else. It's very clear to him, and to anyone else, that you will do whatever is necessary to save the relationship—but to put it mildly, you don't know what to do.

His Agenda:

He doesn't want to work on the relationship, and he doesn't want to change things. He doesn't even want to discuss it because to do so opens up the possibility of resolution. His refusal to do anything that would help the relationship grow is a clear statement of his position.

But all of your complaints and questions make it overwhelmingly apparent to him that the relationship cannot stay the same. Yet he knows he doesn't want it to grow. Simply put: He doesn't want a committed, monogamous relationship.

The Smart Response:

Accept the fact that he doesn't want to work on the relationship. He doesn't want anything to change. Don't act as if he is the one with the problem and you are going to help him. If he wants help, he can find it for himself. Don't point out to him why he should want a more mature relationship. Don't try to convince him how terrific you are. Don't dream up complicated conversational motifs so you can get your points across.

Don't try to get him to acknowledge that he has a problem.

He does have a problem, but you also have a problem. If he doesn't want more between the two of you, all the conversations in the world aren't going to convince him.

The best thing you can do is go your own way. No pushing, prodding, or pleading will do anything. Your absence will say more than a thousand words. If he feels a genuine sense of loss, he may feel differently about change. If he doesn't, there is nothing you could have done anyway. I know this is hard advice to follow, but when a relationship gets this far along without any evidence that it's going to get any better, or more committed, the only sensible thing any woman can do is to leave it and look for something else.

Chapter 10

THE END OF
A COMMITMENTPHOBIC
RELATIONSHIP

THE END

The End phase of a commitmentphobic relationship begins when it becomes apparent to both partners that they can no longer continue without some change taking place. The relationship is falling apart, and only one thing can bring it back together: a commitment from him.

The End is often precipitated by an outside event such as a major holiday, a family wedding, an illness, or a vacation. These events tend to force the commitmentphobic to make a choice: Either he and the woman are together on these occasions, thus acknowledging to the world that he is committed to her, or he excludes her, signifying that they are not really a couple. Unfortunately, even though his guilt or her complaints make him realize that he cannot continue leaving her out, his commitmentphobia doesn't allow him to do anything else.

In the Middle, he was unsure of what he was feeling. Now, at the End, he knows. He feels more anxiety when he's with you than when he's without you. So if a decision has to be made, it's going to be made in favor of ending it.

But, remember, he is, after all, a commitmentphobic. This means he can't make a permanent commitment in either direction, be it to stay or to leave. Consequently, he prefers that it all happen indirectly, with you assuming much of the responsibility.

Everything he does from this point forward, therefore, is directed toward making you aware of the fact that he's leaving—without him actually having to tell you.

Typically, he begins by taking back everything he ever gave you at the Beginning. All the ways he once made you emotionally secure, he now makes you insecure. Remember all the things he did to show you he cared? Well, now it seems as though he will do nothing.

He is also firming up all his escape routes. He may start pushing you to quarrel with him, or he may start behaving so obnoxiously that you will be driven to take some final action. Whatever method he uses, he knows that he will be leaving, but he is not yet sure how he will do it.

You, on the other hand, are probably not reacting appropriately, and even now have the words of the man who said he loved you ringing through your head. He also remembers these words, which is one of the reasons why he is trying to sneak off without an honest discussion.

He is so obviously distressed and unhappy-looking that it's easy to misinterpret what he says. Because you've been through so much together, you may assume that if it hasn't ended by now, it's not going to. The relationship may be so tight, as far as you're concerned, that you're justified in acting like a loyal wife. Typically, therefore, you are putting up with him and acting as though you owe him some form of loyalty. Although you may be fighting with him and pressuring him to change, chances are you are doing little to threaten his sense of security.

In the meantime, he has done so much to threaten your security that your ego may be severely damaged. You are probably alternating between high anxiety and acute depression, and instead of taking care of yourself, you often turn to him, expecting him to make it all better. Usually, this is to no avail.

If the relationship reaches the End, you have almost no leverage left. From my point of view, the best thing you can do is to get out before he does and try to salvage as much self-respect and ego as possible.

The Typical Pattern

1. His attitude toward you has almost totally changed, and he leaves obvious clues that he is on the way out.

Your Typical Response:

Once again, you're in a totally different emotional place than he is. By this stage, you have probably decided that although he has not been making you happy, it's apparent that he doesn't really want to leave you. That tends to intensify your sense of loyalty. You often feel like his wife, even though you both realize that the majority of the problems have been caused because he hasn't been ready to make a commitment. Here's a typical reaction: "I had no idea it was about to end. If anything, I thought we had been through so many ups and downs together that we would probably work it out. I wanted him to make a commitment, but I was prepared to wait if necessary."

His Agenda:

He thinks he's ready to end it, but he feels guilty. He's also torn. Remember, this is a man who can't commit to anything, including *not* making a commitment.

Since he can't confront you and tell you how he feels, he lets you know indirectly. Almost everything he does reflects his inability to take direct action. Here are some of the ways in which he may try to get his message across:

■ He may start talking about moving, leaving town, or taking an extended trip or a vacation—alone.

■ He may leave very obvious clues that he is seeing another woman. (He may, for example, let you catch him in a direct lie.)

■ He may start finding fault with you or picking fights, almost as if to provoke your anger.

■ He may start acting visibly distraught.

■ He may start wanting to spend more time away from you and justify it by saying things such as, "I have to figure out what to do," or "I have to think about us."

As he is doing all of this, he often looks pathetic and confused. Sometimes he is perfectly aware that if you are feeling sorry for him you will be less likely to fight with him about what even he perceives as his weakness. Don't forget that he is just as aware of the way he led you on as you are. He knows that you expect more, but he is hoping that you will feel sorry for him and not make too much of a scene.

The Smart Response:

Now don't go feeling sorry for him because he looks so pathetic and confused. Don't try to be the better, the stronger, or the more mature partner. You are the injured party here, not him.

Often a woman rationalizes the man's behavior and buys his "I have to find myself" speech. When this happens, she assumes an "I will wait for you" pose. This does nothing for her except ultimately make her angry. Behaving like Penelope will not magically turn him into Ulysses.

Instead of wasting any more energy trying to help him find himself, it's time for you to find your luggage and get out of there.

If you reach this point, there is little you can do except cut your emotional losses and exit from the relationship with as much self-respect and ego as you can manage to scrape together.

If he wants to come after you and go into counseling with you, terrific, but hanging around watching him twist and shout isn't going to achieve anything.

2. He spends less time with you and doesn't bother to give you much of an explanation.

Your Typical Response:

Since he hasn't said anything to you directly about wanting to end it—as a matter of fact, he is probably still denying it— you continue to ask him what is going on, and try to believe whatever he tells you. Through this all, you probably wait for his phone calls and are available when he asks to see you.

You may also try to get him to see you more frequently, and often you argue with him about what he's doing or not doing. Typically, you also cry a lot and spend an excessive amount of time trying to analyze what happened.

His Agenda:

To relieve his guilt, he's hoping to get you accustomed to being without him. He thinks that by doing this sort of easing out, he's being considerate. It's almost as if he believes you won't notice.

One man described it to me this way: "It's like we're both together staring at our reflections in a department-store window, and I take two steps back, and I'm gone . . . it was just two steps."

Like you, he remembers the way he was at the Beginning, but he is hoping you will forget. He hopes that he will wake up one morning, and his "reflection" will have disappeared.

The Smart Response:

Don't phone him. Don't write letters. Don't try to prove yourself to him. Don't wait for him. Don't ask to see him. Don't plan meetings in which you try to seduce him. Don't plan parties hoping he will come. In other words, don't twist your life around in a futile attempt to get his attention.

Do forget you ever met this guy. Do start getting your life back together. If it means seeing a therapist, do it. Do get out. Do ask your friends to help keep you busy. Do tell him to get lost if he calls.

Don't think that if you can somehow grab on to him, even for a minute, you will get him to stay. It won't work.

Look, I know you have to go through a mourning period. If you reached this stage, it went too far. But, at the same time, if the relationship seems to be dead, trying to revive it will only rob you of whatever emotional energy you have left.

3. He insists upon flexibility and space.

Your Typical Response:

Still remembering the way he was at the Beginning, you hope that if you go along with everything he says, he will realize that commitment is not that threatening. Since there is little you can do except go along with his "rules," you try to give him the space he requests, but you're not quite sure how.

His Agenda:

Totally sensitized to the notion of commitment, he is over-whelmed by his need for space. The slightest little thing is making him feel trapped. When he is with you, he feels as though he can't breathe. He is yearning for a sense of freedom, and anything you do he perceives as a means of entrapment. Even if you go along with him, he just thinks you are trying to manipulate him into making a commitment. As far as he is concerned, you are his jailer.

The Smart Response:

Realize that you can do nothing right. Don't even tell him that you will give him more "space," because the very idea that you are in a position to control how much or how little "space" he has confirms your jailer status and enrages him.

The only thing you can do is take as much space as possible for yourself, preferably a hundred miles or more. This, of course, is directly opposed to everything you want to do. Right now, you want to work this out with him, but you have to understand that this is not possible.

You are not in an easy position right now, and you are probably feeling a lot of pain and distress. This is the man with whom you may have wanted to build a life. But you have to forget that and get the kind of space you need so you can look at what happened objectively.

Tell him that you both need time and space to think things over. But in reality, *you* are the person who needs time and space, because you are the person who got caught in his madness.

Clean your apartment. Get rid of things that remind you of him. If you can't throw them out, put them in a box, tape it up, and put it in the back of a closet. Think about how much worse off you would be if you had married him.

4. He breaks dates and changes plans.

Your Typical Response:

If you are still with him, you are so confused by the contradictions in his behavior that all you want is an explanation. If he didn't want to see you, why did he make the date? If he doesn't want to talk to you, why does he call? Your judgment is probably awry; your ego is deflated.

You have invested a lot of emotional energy in this man, and all you want is for him to go back to the way he was at the Beginning. But you don't know how to make that happen, so you try all approaches, from cold anger to almost maternal tolerance. Unfortunately, nothing seems to work.

His Agenda:

In his head, he will feel less guilty and confused if he manages to convince you that he doesn't love you—in the same way that he convinced you that he did at the Beginning. It is almost as if he is now trying to take back everything he gave you at the Beginning. Remember some of the feelings he gave you—the sense of security, the sense of being loved, the overwhelming intimacy? Now he wants it all back.

You have to understand, the relationship is so close to commitment that his internal alarm system is ringing so loud he can't hear himself think. So he's not thinking—he's thrashing about, trying to find the exit.

From the men interviewed, it seems fair to say, also, that he is angry at you because you provoked these feelings. He may realize that blaming you is irrational, but that's the way he feels.

The Smart Response:

Recognize what he is doing, and realize that there is nothing you can do or say to "make him change his mind and stay." Don't worry about what he needs to make him feel better. Don't waste your energy thinking about different approaches that might work. The only thing that might work, even now, is distancing yourself. If you try to stay close to him and keep slugging it out, so to speak, you are going to be the one who suffers the most immediate damage. You have to withdraw because it's just a matter of time before he does.

5. He is moody much of the time, but he still blames it on something else; he may go so far as to say, "It's not you."

Your Typical Response:

One of the main reasons a woman gets confused at the End is that she accepts what the commitmentphobic is telling her (just as she did at the Beginning). If you have ever been involved in this situation you know that you believe him because you want to believe him. Perhaps you go so far as to try, once again, to act like the dutiful wife. He says that you're not causing his moods, so you may think that something is seriously wrong. You tend to overdramatize the little conflicts in his life as you look for an explanation. You do everything you can to be understanding and tolerant, no matter how intolerable his behavior.

His Agenda:

Here's what's happening in his head: He has definitely decided to leave you, but he has large question marks over his decision. And, don't forget, he feels guilty—not so guilty that he would change his decision, but guilty nonetheless.

He knows better than anyone that you haven't done anything wrong, and that your only flaw is that you want to be with him in a permanent relationship. He knows that while it's you that's bothering him, it's not you. You have to understand that he doesn't want to discuss this with you because if he did, you might start trying to work it out, and then he would really be stuck.

By this point, he may be seeing another woman. His confusion over what he is doing with her may also be contributing to his moodiness. But whether or not there is another woman, he would like to leave you without you noticing that he's done so. That way, if he changes his mind and wants to come back, everything will go right back to the way it was.

Whatever is going on in his head, he doesn't want you to get any closer. So when you ask what's wrong, he comes up with a dozen other excuses and hopes you will buy one or a combination of them.

The Smart Response:

Don't think you're his wife and have to understand his moods. Besides, since you are feeling the exact opposite of what he is feeling, it's almost impossible for you to step into his shoes and understand. You want to bond, and he wants to separate. This is what is bothering him.

There is probably no other larger-than-life drama going on in his life to justify his moods, so don't imagine romanticized scenarios in which he does have a real problem, and you get to stand by your man.

At this point, I would just assume that he is thinking about another woman, if not actually seeing one. Don't think that his seeing more of you will make her vanish.

You are too far along, and he is too panicked, for you to do anything except try to take yourself and back away. Save your emotional energy to help you get through a very difficult period. Don't waste it on his moods.

6. He still confuses you by what he says and gives very mixed messages: One minute it's harsh rejection or fault finding; the next it's sentimental love or total approval.

Your Typical Response:

When he says something nice to you, you cling to it and hope. When he says or does something rejective, you pray it will go away. You are probably depressed, extraordinarily anxious, insecure, and absolutely miserable.

His Agenda:

Of course he still has feelings for you. Whenever he thinks about leaving you forever, he remembers the good things. They pop up in his mind so often that he can't make a clean break.

He can't even make a commitment to himself that it's over. He can't go forward and he can't go back. So he vacillates.

When he feels guilty, he may say things to make you feel better. He may keep much of the interplay between the two of you limited to phone calls, and he may even make cute little phone calls, almost like he did at the Beginning. This confuses you even more.

These phone calls, by the way, are apt to turn into angry battles because you are trying to pin him down. In the meantime, he is experiencing classic flight or fight symptoms. Away from you, he feels relaxed and misses you—but the slightest contact with you may provoke feelings of entrapment.

He gives confused messages because his feelings are confused.

The Smart Response:

Seeing more of you is not going to make him less confused. All it will do is make him run faster. Don't ask him to explain why he's so contradictory. It's like trying to get an explanation from the IRS.

You may get the sense that he is trying to put you on hold—giving you just enough to keep you in the relationship. Don't make the mistake of interpreting this to mean that he knows what he is doing, and that if you stay in the relationship, he will reward you with his love—he doesn't, and he won't.

If you have reached this point, you are accustomed to so little that you are probably numb from the way he has destroyed your ego. Don't be embarrassed by this, because it has happened to many, many other women. It's unfortunate, but true. You have to do whatever is necessary to break away emotionally in as positive and healthy a fashion as possible. I know this is easier said than done, but you have to try.

You can't make the mistake of regarding the intimacy that existed between you as friendship. Don't expect him to be your best friend or to take care of you emotionally. You have to do it for yourself. Don't sit by your phone waiting for his calls, clinging to the belief that as long as you are there for him, he will not go away from you. This is not going to work.

You have to accept the fact that he is no longer emotionally available to you, and you have to make sure that you are not emotionally available to him.

7. He withdraws sexually and blames it on work, fatigue, or illness. He implies that if you were really understanding, you would understand.

Your Typical Response:
This feels like the last step in the rejection process, and you are hurt, betrayed, and confused. Unfortunately, you probably still want him and love him.

His Agenda:
Total sexual withdrawal is usually what he saves for last. He doesn't want to go to bed with you because he's worked too hard at detaching. He's afraid that if he sleeps with you, it will be misinterpreted, and you will think the relationship is improving. His decision not to sleep with you is a conscious decision. He will probably tell you that he is having some sort of other emotional problem, and indicate that his sexual withdrawal is temporary. This way the door is not completely closed.

The Smart Response:

Would it help any if I told you that almost every woman interviewed had had first-hand experience with this kind of sexual rejection? It seems to be a fairly standard commitmentphobic procedure.

Whatever you do, don't try to seduce him, and don't try to change his mind. Here's why:

■ If you try to seduce him and it fails, which it probably will, you will feel even worse.

■ Those women who did manage to seduce the man at this point reported that he took flight almost immediately afterward, ending the relationship for good.

This is his problem—don't make it yours. Don't feel rejected, and don't feel a need to prove yourself. Be kind to yourself and stay away from him.

8. He won't do anything at all to try to improve the relationship—he won't even talk about it.

Your Typical Response:

You still think you can talk to him.

His Agenda:

He doesn't want to do anything; he doesn't want to talk about anything. Talking about the problem only intensifies the problem, because it makes him worry that you may find a way to work this thing out. In his head, he's like a guy on Death Row, and you keep offering to help fix the electric chair. I know that sounds a bit extreme, but believe me, that's how he's thinking.

The Smart Response:

There's nothing to discuss. You've got to start working on your life. Don't make threats, just do it. Take his refusal to work on the relationship with you for what it is—a refusal to work on the relationship. Get out. Get away.

Do whatever you have to do to get your priorities in order, and make sure he is not one of them. And remember one thing: If he is a commitmentphobic, it was not your fault.

Chapter 11 _____

THE BITTER END OF A COMMITMENTPHOBIC RELATIONSHIP

THE BITTER END

I hope most of you never get to this point. However, if you do, it may help if you realize that the man who is making you so miserable is not that "special." He is a commitmentphobic with a discernible pattern and recognizable tactics. Recognizing his tactics, and his antics, for what they are may not erase the pain you feel, but it should help you recognize a "no win" situation for what it is.

The Bitter End is the worst-case commitmentphobic's final theater piece. If you are unfortunate enough to be involved with a man who brings you to this point, keep in mind that no matter what he tells you, how he beats his chest, or whatever other form of histrionics he employs, he is not Laurence Olivier, and the only Oscar he'll receive is for special effects.

I'm not trying to be overly flip here, and I think it's inappropriate to mask your unhappiness with humor. He's made you miserable, and you have a right to feel miserable. But I do think you will be better able to quickly get on with your life if you recognize this man's melodrama for what it is—yet another way of avoiding commitment.

He Can't Stay, but He Also Won't Commit Himself to Leaving

If you need any further proof that the man is a commitment-phobic, take a look at the way he leaves relationships. He can't commit himself to leaving any more easily than he can to staying. End result: Even at the Bitter End, he is giving mixed and distorted messages—he seems almost incapable of giving you an honest, straightforward statement of either his feelings or his intentions.

Why It Ends

It ends because when he's with you, he feels as though he is gasping for air. He may still love you, but he has no sense of freedom, and freedom is what he craves. By the time your relationship hits the Bitter End, the commitmentphobic is out of control. He is so sensitized to what you represent that he can't deal with you in any way that resembles normal behavior. He's like an acrophobic being dangled by his feet over the edge of the Empire State Building. As far as he's concerned, all you're doing is trying to tickle his toes. He just wants his discomfort to end.

LESS THAN FIFTY WAYS TO LEAVE A LOVER

The typical worst-case commitmentphobic ends relationships in one—or a combination—of three possible ways: He *provokes* you into ending it; he *withdraws* slowly to the point where there is no relationship left; he *disappears*.

Whichever way he chooses, he often manages to get you, the woman who loves him, to accept one—or all—of the following roles:

> Mother
> Therapist
> Best Friend

When you assume these roles, you are asked to put his emotional well-being above yours. Thus he becomes the more important person in the relationship.

Here's how this works: You as Mother are packing his bags for him, while you as Therapist are asking him if he is sure he knows where he wants to go, and you as Best Friend are driving him to the airport.

When this happens, your needs are obliterated—lost in the confusion. Somehow everything is turned around, and he uses these ways to keep you close to him until he no longer needs you and firmly shuts the door. In the meantime, you typically can't believe—considering everything you have shared—that it will ever be over. Only after he is gone does the reality become depressingly clear. Your confusion often continues indefinitely, making the recovery period doubly difficult.

Three Ways a Commitmentphobic Leaves a Lover

1. He provokes you into ending it by starting a huge argument or engaging in particularly outrageous behavior.

Your Typical Response:
"I can't believe what I put up with. He began seeing other women and saw more and more of them and less and less of me. But when I would ask him if he wanted to split up, he would always say no. Through this all, I never knew when I would see him—it was like going out with a married man. I tried breaking up a couple of times, but he told me he loved me and said he didn't know why I put up with him. I would cry and ask him if he wanted to break up, and he always said no. He sort of implied he needed more time. He called me every day, and I thought he would change. One day I called his house and a woman answered and said he was in the shower. I felt too humiliated . . . I just couldn't take any more. I refused to see him—and this time it took."

Typically, when the commitmentphobic finally pushes you over the edge, you are at your wit's end. You are too unhappy, too disgusted, and too discouraged to continue one minute longer. You've finally had it, and you tell him so. No sooner does he close the door than you start crying and wondering whether you did the right thing. Now you're without him. What will you do? All you can think about is how to get him back. You remember the way he was at the Beginning and wonder what you did to make him stop loving you.

His Agenda:

In his heart of hearts, he knows you can't put up with it forever, and he just pushes until you reach the breaking point. Whether he is totally conscious of this, or only partially conscious, the motivation is the same: He wants to leave, but he wants you to take responsibility. Men know what will bring a woman to the point of no return. It's often behavior over which there have been many battles in the past. Some typical examples:

"I brought Joan to Donna's apartment and made love to her when Donna was at work. Of course Donna found out. Donna said what she minded most was that I let Joan wear her bathrobe. I can't believe I was that stupid."

"I was amazingly flagrant about my affairs, and eventually she found out and retaliated justifiably."

"I left her on New Year's Eve and went to a party at my sister's house without taking her. I knew she would explode, and she did."

"I criticized her all the time—I don't know why—I was definitely the more controlled of the two of us. One night she made dinner for my birthday. She obviously went to a lot of trouble, and she got me three presents I really liked. We made love after dinner. Afterward, I went into the kitchen. She had left the dirty dessert dishes with the birthday cake on a counter. I pointed out to her how it always upset me to find dirty dishes. She got furious, and stormed out. I'm sure she could have found time to wash them if she really wanted to. It's probably just as well we split up—we were too different."

"I didn't take her to my cousin's wedding."

"I rented a new apartment, and for some reason I didn't want to let her see it. I don't know why—but I just didn't want her there. She finally showed up at my door one night, and when I opened it, she threw all the clothes I kept in her apartment on the floor."

The Smart Response:

Don't regret your decision for a moment. Know that he wanted you to do it. It was not your fault, and he provoked you. The only thing you should be upset about is that you didn't do it sooner.

When you reach this point, you should also be careful about doing something that will make you feel like a total fool. If you're going to ultimately feel humiliated because you "lost it" in public, watch out. This man's behavior could cause a saint to act like a madwoman.

2. He withdraws so totally (he may even move) that the relationship dies of attrition.

Your Typical Response:

"We went through all the stages . . . insane breakups, fights, reconciliations . . . but finally it ended because it sort of wore down to nothing. He took everything away and then there was nothing left. He started seeing less of me, with a lot of reasons why. Then he took a summer house—with friends—and said there wasn't room for guests, including me. I would say that it was obvious that he didn't want to see me anymore, but he would deny it. It took us about a year to wind down to the point where there was nothing left. We just saw less and less of each other. I don't even remember the actual ending."

Somehow his behavior gradually conditions you to expect less and less. You act like a wife whose devoted husband is on an extended trip. Through it all, because he somehow made it clear that you were the woman in his life, you expect it to change. When it doesn't, you are often so accustomed to staying home waiting for his calls or his visits that you no longer have a real life.

His Agenda:

Because he is simply too guilty to end it, he hopes the relationship will eventually evaporate. He gives just enough to keep it alive and not a drop more. To you, he has every excuse to justify what he does:

"I don't know . . . I need more time. . . ."

"I've got to see how my job works out . . . a lot depends on the promotion."

"I'm too young to settle down . . . maybe next year. . . ."

"I'm too old . . . I don't know if I can do it now . . . but then again, tomorrow I might feel different."

"I know the new job is a thousand miles away, but that doesn't mean we can't see each other."

This man's theme song is always "Tomorrow." This does not, however, mean that he seriously expects to change tomorrow. It just means that he is *incapable* of actually ending the relationship. He expects you to catch his drift and know that nothing is going to change—except for the worse. When you continue to hang in there, he feels no responsibility whatsoever for your behavior. Although he may realize that you have put your life on hold while you wait for him to come to his senses, he doesn't feel that this obligates him to change.

This sort of withdrawal is often a built-in component of long-distance relationships, where it's very easy for the man over a period of time to see less and less of the woman.

The Smart Response:

Don't waste any more of your precious time with this man. Even smart women have wasted years waiting for men like this to make up their minds. When a man backs away gradually like this, a woman is often paralyzed by the fact that she has no power in the relationship that is eroding around her. This paralysis often affects everything she does. Consequently, she does nothing. This is not the time for you to give up your life. Force yourself to go out, make plans, and look for new relationships.

Many women need to feel that there is some resolution. They

just want the man to tell them that the relationship is over. Somehow that's the only way they feel free enough to go out again. If this is the case, you are going to have to be the one to end it. Unfortunately, that is also difficult to do. As one woman said to me, "How can I call him up and tell him it's over, when it doesn't really exist? Yet, at the same time, I feel as though he expects me to be there, and I keep waiting for him."

When this happens, you must force yourself to stop waiting and dreaming. Forget every romantic notion, and work on practical ways of dealing with life. If you need a therapist to help you break away from him emotionally, by all means find one. But make sure you don't use therapy as a means of continuing to talk about or obsess about what might have been.

3. He stops calling, doesn't return your phone calls, and totally disappears from your life, often in a way that is bizarre as well as destructive.

Your Typical Response:

"This is terrible, but it's what happened. We were supposed to be engaged, but he started dating someone at work so I ended it. Then he showed up at my door sobbing and saying how sorry he was and how much he loved me. I believed him and we started seeing each other again. Then, two weeks later, over Thanksgiving, he didn't call me, and I couldn't reach him on the phone. I went to his house, and he wasn't home. I was worried sick. . . . I thought for sure something awful had happened to him. I kept calling and calling. I got him at work on Monday. He told me he couldn't see me anymore because he and an old girlfriend had decided to try living together. Believe it or not, I was still worried sick. I thought he was having a complete breakdown . . . I even called his mother . . ."

Typically, when a man disappears this way, you alternate between worry and anger. One day you were together, the next he was gone. You don't understand why he didn't have the decency to confront you and talk to you about what he was feeling. You don't understand why he is treating you so badly. You don't understand any of it. Hence, you decide he must have lost his sanity and his good sense. Often you deny what has happened, and keep expecting him to go back to the way he was.

It may take a long time to recover from this experience. Not only do you feel betrayed, but often there is a dreamlike quality to everything that's taking place. It just doesn't seem real. How could he drop you so quickly?

Often you try to phone him to get him to say something, give you some kind of explanation. or you may try to see him. If there is another woman involved, which there often is, you worry about phoning him when she might be there. You keep hoping you will wake up and discover it didn't happen. In the meantime, you try to think up ways to reestablish the old bond between the two of you.

His Agenda:

He knows that he has taken the relationship as far as he can go. He can't go any further. Yet he has gone too far. He can see no way to have a conversation with you about what he is feeling. He feels like a prisoner, and escape, to him, is the only way out. This doesn't mean that he doesn't like you. It's just that he pushed the relationship too far, and it's not what he wants.

But no one is more acutely aware than he of how he led you on. Consequently, he is overwhelmed with a combination of guilt and anxiety. He understands precisely why you expect and deserve more from him. Because he realizes this is completely his doing, he can't confront you. What would he say?

So he handles his guilt by not seeing you and not confronting you. He hopes that by pretending you don't exist—wiping you out, at least temporarily—his guilt will disappear. Here are some typical reactions:

"I just couldn't take it any further. I felt bad—I knew I should call her, but I couldn't bring myself to do it. So I put it off. Every day I put it off made it more impossible for me to ever do so."

"I had gotten myself in way too far, and it seemed like the only way out. I buried myself with the way I chased her. I know a "real man" would have given some explanation, but it would have seemed so ludicrous. How could I explain that to someone who I had been so intimate with—how could I say that was it? Call it cowardice, call it what you want. I just couldn't face her."

"I just woke up one day and realized what I had done. No question about it—I didn't want to get married. I didn't even want to see her again."

The Smart Response:

The first thing to understand is that this man is a type. I call him Houdini, after the showman who couldn't be tied or bound. A Houdini is particularly destructive because he is almost always the one who insisted upon being tied up. Once you do what he asks, he disappears. When he reappears, he is totally different, or he has another woman, a stage assistant, with him. A Houdini escape is most common in short, intense commitmentphobic relationships. Houdini got in over his head too soon, and he just had to get out.

Recognize the type, and understand that he is the most destructive of the commitmentphobics. When he first disappears, you must immediately realize all of the following: He is not dead. He is not lying in a gutter crying your name. He has not been kidnapped by a small, unfriendly nation with no phones. He is gone because he wants to be gone, and he's a creep.

Don't wait for him to call you again. Don't think he is having a nervous breakdown from which he will emerge his old loving self. Don't do anything that has anything to do with him. Every second you waste thinking about him, talking about him, or talking to him will only cause you more pain.

Giving up him—and the idea of him—is harder than giving up cigarettes, but it must be done. The sooner you do it, the sooner you can get back to your own life.

If this happens to you, realize that it has happened to many, many, many other women. Don't be embarrassed by it. Don't keep telling yourself that he really loved you. Don't romanticize his problems and his conflict. Don't give yourself an important role in his life.

More survival hints:

- Resist the tendency to dramatize your plight—or his.
- Resist wallowing in your pain—it will just last longer.

- Don't keep thinking about all the things he said to you.
- Don't obsess about what you could have done, should have done, or might have done.
- Don't obsess about all the ways he hurt you.
- Stop thinking about what might have been.
- Get some satisfaction from the fact that this will never, ever, happen to you again because now you know what to do.

CURTAIN CALLS

It's finally over. You slowly start to put your life back together. It's time to forget about him and go on. Although there is a lot of pain and hurt, the worst of it seems to have passed. But suddenly a letter arrives, or the phone rings, or there is a knock on the door. It's him—again. He's despondent, miserable, desperate.

It was a terrible mistake, he tells you, the biggest mistake of his life. He can't stand the thought of never seeing you again. He asks you to please accept his apologies—give him another chance. He promises it will be different . . . better. You're stunned. You've just started to heal, and now all the wounds are opening. Everything is rushing back. You can hardly believe your ears—it's everything you wanted to hear.

STOP RIGHT HERE. Ask yourself what's going on. What's he thinking?

Well, the sad truth is that he is probably *not* thinking. It's the Beginning all over again. As soon as he left you, the worst part of his problem was over. Without the anxiety, without the fear, he was free to miss you—to remember all the good things about you, and to stop looking for the bad. So he's back. But what does this really mean?

It means nothing. He is the same man he always was. He may start pursuing you, exactly as he did at the Beginning. Typically, he repeats the entire relationship, going through all of the steps. Only this time, it's in a much more condensed, faster version.

If he wants to see a couples counselor, you may have a chance. However, from everyone I've talked to, if he comes to this point after taking you through all the aforementioned stages, it is highly unlikely he will be able to overcome his commitment-phobic problems. As a matter of fact, he has probably set a pattern for himself, making it that much easier for him to repeat it the second time around.

THESE FOOLISH THINGS—COMMITMENTPHOBIC MEMORABILIA

Another odd little detail that many women have mentioned: After the relationship is over, the man often refuses, or neglects, to return her belongings. She may, for example, have left articles of clothing or books or records in his apartment. Merilee, a designer, was totally baffled by her ex-boyfriend's behavior:

"Larry left me for another woman, and I gave him no grief over it—even though the way he did it was totally rotten. However, I had left a couple of nightgowns, my favorite hat, and a jacket at his apartment. Also, two nights before he told me he didn't want to see me anymore, I loaned him fifty dollars because his bank machine wasn't working and mine was. Well, now he won't return any of it. He makes ten times more money than I do, but that's not even the point. My things are my things, and under the circumstances, I resent his keeping my money. I would think he would be so guilty he would send me the money at least, but he won't. I've tried everything reasonable. I sent a note. I sent him a stamped self-addressed jiffy bag so he could just pop it in the mail. He won't do it, and I don't know why."

Here's why he won't return your stuff. You know the old saying, "It's not really over until it's over"? Well, in his twisted, convoluted way of thinking, your belongings are his lifeline to you. He knows it, and he knows you know it. He's cast you adrift, but that doesn't necessarily mean that he wants you to land on a foreign shore. Truth told, he would like it if you waited for him. Wait for what? He has no idea. Maybe a bolt of lightning will strike him someday, and he will change his mind. If it does, he has an excuse to get hold of you again. Once again, this is a clear example of his inability to commit—either way.

Chapter 12

HOW TO AVOID A COMMITMENTPHOBIC RELATIONSHIP— RULES TO LIVE BY

RULE #1: KNOW YOU DON'T THINK THE WAY HE DOES

It's easy to assume that the commitmentphobic thinks the same way that you do—but he doesn't. The kinds of things that make you feel secure make him feel suffocated. Some of the things you perceive as love, he perceives as entrapment. Too often a commitmentphobic runs because a woman is only giving him what she thinks he wants. This kind of emotional catering doesn't work, and it's time you worried more about what *you* want.

RULE #2: YOU SET THE PACE

Regardless of how tempting it is to let him sweep you off your feet and take total control, *you* must control the pace of the relationship—it is the only to avoid the typical commitment-phobic scenario. He wants a whirlwind romance—fast and furious. But only slow and steady relationship growth will be able to set the foundation for permanency. And the key word here is slow. If it goes too fast, he will get frightened. It's that simple. It's important to be slow to open up, slow to accept him, slow to give your trust, slow to reach the bedroom. Keep reminding yourself that if this is going to be the romance of the century, you'll have a century in which to enjoy it. Therefore, you won't be missing much by keeping a tight grip on the reins, and you may be gaining everything. If he can't handle your slower pace, it's all the more indication that he's not in this for the long haul.

RULE #3: REALITY, NOT FANTASY

We all want a storybook romance, but as you have probably learned by now, too many of these romances have unhappy endings. The commitmentphobic is often a hopeless romantic who is lost in a fantasy world and trying desperately to get you to join him. You can't buy his fantasy, regardless of how appealing it is—and it will be appealing—because it is only a fantasy. Sooner or later, all fantasies have to end, and with a commitment-phobic, it's usually sooner. A solid relationship begins, grows, and matures in reality. This is true even though reality is often not nearly as appealing (and how could it be?). If you start losing control of yourself and your emotions, stop immediately, and get yourself on a more realistic track—fast.

RULE #4: UNDERSTAND THAT YOUR LOVE WON'T CHANGE HIM—YOUR INDEPENDENCE MIGHT

There is a myth believed by many women, fostered by films of the forties and romance novels of the eighties, that the love of a good woman can conquer any obstacle. The average woman was taught to believe that if she loved enough, she would eventually be rewarded for her efforts. Loving enough means being perfectly faithful, loyal, supportive, etc. Stand by your man, and he will realize how much he needs you. It works in the movies, but it doesn't work in real life. He saw the same movies you did, and appreciates your attempts to overwhelm him with love—but *overwhelm* is the operative word here. All this abundance of love does is make him feel overwhelmed with fear.

Your independence, on the other hand, allows him to breathe. Independence and love are not mutually exclusive, but to a commitmentphobic, the minute a woman showers him with "love," he thinks he's drowning.

RULE #5: TO MOTHER IS TO SMOTHER

It's easy to feel sorry for this guy. He often seems so sensitive and confused. Like a kid. What he needs is a little maternal care, right? Wrong. The minute you start worrying about his comfort, his sleep, his psychological well-being, or his tummy, you are treading on phobic territory. When he feels mothered, he feels smothered. Don't do it.

Note: It's easy to get into the habit of making dinner for him, cleaning up after him, and generally letting him avoid all household unpleasantries in the same way his mother did in his youth. Don't. He's a full partner in this relationship— let him act like one.

RULE #6: NO PLAYING HOUSE

If you're not married, don't act as though you are. What does that mean? Simple. Don't let him get into the habit of treating you like a wife while he acts like a sometime guest.

Here's how this works. You, looking forward to seeing him, don't ask for anything more. You really don't mind cooking dinner and having a quiet evening at home. But what often happens is that a vicious pattern is established. You end up trotting out all your wifely skills—almost as if you had nothing to do all day except to prepare for him. In the meantime, he arrives with that "I'm exhausted" look on his face, and while he hangs off the couch watching the tube, you do your Donna Reed/Marabel Morgan imitation. And the worst part is that he actually walks away with the impression that you really *didn't* have anything better to do all day than to cater to him. This, of course, makes him very uncomfortable.

This is just a bad, inequitable setup. And often the woman is just as responsible as, if not more responsible than, the man.

Playing house is counter-productive.

RULE #7: BELIEVE WHAT HE DOES, NOT WHAT HE SAYS

The commitmentphobic is a man of many words, but few actions. Learn to differentiate between the two. Although you want to believe his words, you shouldn't act on them or (heaven forbid) change your life because of them, until he backs these words up with real and *enduring* substance. If he doesn't, you must accept the fact that his words were just words.

RULE #8: KEEP YOUR OPTIONS OPEN

An uncommitted man is an uncommitted man, regardless of what you think or hope he can or will eventually become. You cannot cut yourself off socially—i.e., from other men—assuming he will eventually give you the commitment you desire. Granted, dating and socializing can be extremely unpleasant at times, and it is often far easier to sit home, watch television, and think about the man you love. But this kind of social isolation is counter-productive, and can often be destructive. So unless you have a firm commitment from him, never reject an opportunity to broaden your social horizons. And if he gets jealous? Let him do something about it.

RULE #9: DON'T FIND EXCUSES FOR HIS BEHAVIOR

He had a troubled childhood . . . he has a difficult mother . . . he wasn't loved enough . . . he was loved too much . . . his job is too stressful . . . his job isn't challenging . . . he had a bad first marriage . . . he had a bad second marriage, etc., etc. You can always find a good excuse to accept the behavior of a commitmentphobic man. But almost *every* man had some major problems in his life and so for that matter, has almost every woman. And many men with far greater personal stress don't treat women the way the commitmentphobic does. His psychological problems may be influencing his commitmentphobic behavior, but they don't justify that behavior. If he is hurting you his behavior is inexcusable, regardless of its determinants, and it isn't your place to play amateur psychiatrist. In short, don't accept or try to explain away behavior that is unacceptable.

RULE #10: DON'T TAKE THE BLAME FOR THE FAILURE OF A COMMITMENTPHOBIC RELATIONSHIP

When a relationship fails, well-intentioned women find it all too easy to accept the blame and responsibility. However, when the man is a commitmentphobic you must remember that his problem is not your problem. His relationships fail because of his internal turmoil—not because you are a bad partner. Some of these men are so good at destroying relationships that they are like hardened professionals. Don't take the rap and send yourself to jail for his crime.

RULE #11: TAKE CARE OF YOU

Most important of all, never forget the fact that the most important person in your life is *YOU*—now and always. He will take care of himself. You must take care of you. You have your needs, your work, your friends, your family, your priorities, and you must always attend to them. You can't let yourself be so swallowed up into his world that you lose sight of the woman who attracted him in the first place.

You need space—physical and emotional—and so does he. You need independence, and so does he. Don't expect him to give up his space and independence, and whatever you do, don't give up yours. Sure, some compromise is necessary, but that requires that both parties agree to compromise for the good of the relationship and both parties compromise.

Don't be afraid that your independence and self-protectiveness offend him, alienate him, or turn him off. He may complain about it, but believe me if you take care of yourself (which is better for you anyway) you are *less* likely to trigger his commitment-phobic anxieties.

RULE #12: DON'T SAY, "I CAN'T CHANGE"

One final word of advice: All too often, I'll meet a woman who's at the end of a particularly hurtful relationship with a man who can't commit and she will tell me, "I can't change. Someday

I'll find a man who appreciates the way I am—who will love me for all the right reasons." Sometimes this same woman will then meet another man, be just as trusting, just as vulnerable, just as willing to go along with his scenario, and get hurt once again.

I have recommended a fair number of changes which I feel are crucial for relationship growth. But when I talk about making changes, I am not talking about altering fundamental qualities that make you who you are. I don't want to suggest that you, or any woman, change the core that defines you. If anything I'm only asking that you take better care of that core.

Ironically, the same women who say they can't change are the ones who change too much in an effort to become the perfect lover/wife/mother figure that the commitmentphobic appears to want. In other words, they stop acting like themselves when they get involved in a relationship. If you are one of these women, you have to recognize that you *do* change—in a negative way.

Instead, I'm asking you to make the kind of smarter, positive changes that allow you to protect yourself. This does not mean that you have to become less loving, less sincere, more manipulative, less feminine. It just means that you have to take care of the qualities you cherish and not rush into any relationship until you know that they will be valued. Trust your instincts and be cautious. If you build your relationship slowly and sensibly, you are infinitely more likely to find a committed, long-term love.

APPENDIX

IF HE ASKS FOR HELP: A Guide to Treating Commitmentphobia

In a perfect world, any relationship would be a fifty-fifty prop-
osition with both partners making an equal effort to work through
their difficulties. Unfortunately, when it comes to a problem like
commitmentphobia many men are not inclined to make such an
effort. You see, unfortunately many of these men don't really
want to change—at least not that much. It's not that these men
are entirely in love with their lifestyle—often they are quite
lonely and depressed. It's just that the alternative—commitment
—seems far worse. For this reason, I have focused until this
point on what *you* can do about the problem.

But some men do want to change, or at least to try to change
especially if they are involved with a woman they don't want to
lose. Perhaps you can recall a time when a man expressed this
desire to you (probably through tear-filled eyes). Unfortunately,
you probably didn't have the vaguest idea what to tell him, so
you sat back and hoped that his desire to change would be
enough. But it wasn't.

Just because a man expresses a desire to do something about
his problem with commitment you cannot assume that he is
capable of making any positive changes on his own. Nor can you
interpret this as a signal for you to assume the role of therapist
and try to change him. You should *never* try to change him, you
can only change the way you interact with him in order to protect
and take care of yourself. But if he really is willing to do some-

thing about his problem, professional help is available from a variety of experienced therapists.

In this chapter I will briefly summarize the special type of help that is available for phobics. But a word of warning: This chapter is intended to offer *him* an opportunity to do something about his problem. *You* cannot drag him to a therapist, nor can *you* make his appointments. *He* must take the initiative; he must go because *he* wants to go; *he* must assume responsibility for his own change. All you can do is help steer him in the right direction, be supportive of his efforts, and wish him well.

PHOBIC THERAPY: A VARIETY OF APPROACHES

Throughout this book I have asserted that commitmentphobia is a true phobia, complete with all of the physical and psychological symptomatology. I have also offered considerable evidence to support this assertion. But if we are dealing with a true phobia, then we must treat it accordingly. In other words, I think that with a problem such as this just any old therapy will not do; to insure the greatest chance of success, in my opinion commitmentphobia must be approached and treated like a real phobia.

There is no single method for treating all phobias. A variety of therapeutic approaches exists, each with its merits and demerits. While some of these techniques have yet to be applied to the treatment of commitmentphobia, there is no reason to believe that they can't be just as effective as they are for treating any other phobia. In the few pages that follow, you will find a brief summary of the most popular styles of phobic therapy. It is not my place here to pass judgment on these different styles; I only wish to make you aware of your options. The "right" approach, for any man, is the one he finds most comfortable and, hopefully, most helpful.

Psychoanalysis/Psychotherapy

The psychoanalytic approach to treating phobias is based upon the assumption that phobias develop when displaced anxiety suddenly surfaces. This anxiety, according to psychoanalytic the-

ory, stems from unresolved, repressed emotional conflicts—
typically from childhood— of a sexual and/or aggressive nature.

The analyst believes that if these conflicts are uncovered and
resolved, the phobia will dissolve. Therefore, the job of the
analyst is to help the patient probe deep into his or her emotional
past in search of these buried conflicts and to help the patient
come to terms with these conflicts once they are revealed.

While strict psychoanalysis can take many years, various modified psychotherapeutic techniques often produce positive re-
sults within a relatively short period of time.

Behavior Modification

Behavior therapists believe that the best way to treat phobias
is to treat the symptoms, not the alleged source of those symptoms. The theory behind the various behavioral techniques is
that phobic anxiety can be reduced or eliminated if a patient is
continually exposed to the source of his or her fear (in controlled
circumstances, of course). The most popular behavioral techniques are as follows:

Systematic Desensitization

The goal of systematic desensitization is to shrink anxiety through
a process of continuous confrontation and positive reinforcement. When patients undergo systematic desensitization, the
first thing they learn is how to suppress their anxiety with deep
breathing, meditation, muscle control, and other relaxation techniques. Next, the patient is asked to rank a series of fearful
situations in order to develop a hierarchy of his or her fears.

Working with the therapist the patient is instructed to imagine
each of these scenarios, one at a time, in order of increasing
fearfulness. At each step, the various relaxation techniques are
used to neutralize any anxiety. If the patient becomes uncon-
trollably anxious at any point, he is instructed to return to a less
frightening scenario, relax, and proceed forward once again.
Eventually, the patient should be able to imagine the most fearful scenario and still remain calm. This process is repeated over
and over to reinforce that sense of calm. Ultimately, it is hoped
that the patient will reach the point where he is capable of

actually confronting these scenarios wihtout becoming anxious or panicky.

For a man who fears commitment, his relationship hierarchy (remember, he probably has other commitment fears as well), going from least frightening to most frightening, might look something like this:

> Being introduced to a woman
> Asking a woman out for the first time
> Going on a first date
> Having several dates with the same woman
> Sleeping with a woman
> Having a monogamous relationship
> Living together
> Getting engaged
> Getting married
> Having a family

In Vivo Desensitization

For many phobics, in vivo desensitization is an even more effective way to neutralize phobic anxiety. With this method, instead of visualizing the scenarios in the fear hierarchy, the patient is encouraged to actually place himself in these situations and slowly work his way up the ladder. If this method were used to treat commitmentphobia, the therapist would probably encourage the patient to slowly work his way through the many steps that lead to a committed, monogamous relationship (with the woman's cooperation, of course).

As in systematic desensitization, relaxation techniques are used with in vivo desensitization to help control the anxiety response at each level in the hierarchy.

Flooding and Implosion

Two other popular behavioral therapies are flooding and implosion. The theory behind these two forms of behavior modification is that the best way to overcome fear is to face it head on and feel it, rather than to neutralize it.

In flooding therapy the patient, under the therapist's supervision, is encouraged to directly confront his or her phobic "trigger" for a prolonged period of time. If a man is afraid of commitment, the therapist might encourage him to meet that fear head on by immersing himself in a monogamous relationship (once again, with the woman's cooperation). Avoidance or escape are discouraged. It is hoped that the anxiety will eventually burn itself out and the patient will no longer be fearful.

In implosion therapy the therapist makes patients face their fears by verbally frightening them for a prolonged period. Crying or refusing to continue with the session is not permitted since both are considered attempts to escape. Theoretically, the end result of implosion should be the same result anticipated from flooding therapy: anxiety burnout, exhaustion, and no more fear.

Additional Behavioral Techniques

Other behavior modification techniques include hypnotherapy, deep breathing and relaxation exercises, modeling therapy, and biofeedback. The possible benefits of each of these techniques is something the commitmentphobic should discuss with his therapist.

Medication

A growing body of evidence suggests that most, if not all, phobias have at least some *physio*logical component—be it chemical, vestibular, or based on some other unknown factor(s). It has even been suggested that certain individuals have a physiologically determined phobic predisposition—a hypersensitive anxiety mechanism that makes them far more susceptible to these problems. [For more on this, you may want to read *The Anxiety Disease* by Dr. David Sheehan (Scribner, 1983) and *Phobia Free* by Dr. Harold Levinson with Steven Carter (Evans, 1986).]

In light of this, it should not be surprising to learn that many psychiatrists are having great success treating a variety of phobias with medications and dietary supplements. The viability of this treatment approach is something to be discussed with one or more qualified physicians, and no medical therapy should ever be undertaken unless it is under the direction and supervision of a qualified physician.